When I'm With You

A 40-Day
Devotional Challenge

LaVon Chancy

DEDICATION

At all times and in all things, the glory and honor goes to God for His unspeakable gift in the person of Jesus Christ, my savior and friend.

To the first *Fire New* book club! Thank you all for sharing your time and insight with me. Thank you for supporting and encouraging the gifts that God has given me. Without knowing it, you've pushed me to be better. A very special thank you to my sisters, Syreeta, Beatrice, Beverly, Gloria, Sharon and Cheryl—you ladies rock.

And of course my Tribe. Too many to name each one, but you know who you are. I couldn't do this without your love, prayers and support.

Thank you!

TABLE OF CONTENTS

INTRODUCTION

When *I'm With You* is a 40-Day Devotional Challenge to show readers how the word of God affects everyday life situations. Using some of my favorite passages of scripture, I describe the lessons God shared with me pertaining to those verses. In *When I'm With You* I give readers a peek inside my quiet time with God, and I share some of the things God lays on my heart as I meditate on the word of God. That quiet time can be while lying in bed, taking a walk or even driving in my car. The Lord is always speaking to each of us during everyday occurrences. Are you listening to hear Him in the birds singing outside your window, in the wind blowing through the trees, or in the silence of the night? In a story-telling, easy-to-read fashion, I've put together a devotional that will have you pondering God's word each day of the month and beyond. You'll be encouraged, challenged, motivated and inspired to spend time with God each day so that He can share His heart with you as you go through *When I'm With You.*

Whether you're a new Christian or a seasoned saint, whether you're male or female, whether you're young or old, *When I'm With You* is sure to get you engaged in reading and meditating on God's word. The Bible is a fascinating book full of ordinary people doing extraordinary things. As you read this devotional, have a pen handy to jot down what the Holy Spirit shares with you. Meditate on the scriptures throughout the day. Write down your thoughts pertaining to the day's passage. It's my desire that you too will see how practical the word of God is, so that you'll run to it more often to find out what it says about life's issues.

DAY 1:
OUR TIME

(Key Passage: Psalm 16:1-11)

*"You will show me the path of life;
in Your presence is fullness of joy; at Your
right hand are pleasures forevermore."*

Psalm 16:11 (New King James Version)

One of the things I love about springtime is the sound of birds chirping in the morning. Almost every day I'm awakened to lots of chirps or coos or sometimes what sounds almost like screams of birds. They sound so happy to be alive, so carefree, so joyous. The sun isn't even up yet and they're singing what sounds like love songs to one another. Hearing the sounds of those birds, stirs me to get up out of bed, go into my office (which is where I pray) and sit with God.

I read that birds can sing any time of day, but during the dawn hours their songs are louder, livelier and more frequent. And that it's mostly the male birds attempting to attract mates—it's their love call. Hearing them makes me think of God calling me. Waking me up with His love song, wooing me, attracting me into His presence. What an awesome feeling to know that the God of the Universe wants to spend time with little ol' me. That He would care to hear what's on my heart, and better yet, desires to share His heart with me. Oh how I love our time together.

It was during one of our times together that this devotional was put on my heart. I've never been a really good sleeper. I sleep very lightly, so the slightest noise can awaken me. It can be a car driving past our house, my husband moving around in the bed or the sound of a couple of drips from the shower head. So during the night I'm lying down for rest, but I'm usually not sleeping all night. But that's when God speaks to me. Very often it's a song He puts on my heart, or someone to pray for. And every now and then He gives me insight into a passage of scripture, or a thought about His word that I've never considered before. So that I don't lose it, I'll reach for my phone to put it in the Notes section. Sometimes I record the entire message He gives me; others I jot down a few key things and in the morning I'll write it all out in a notebook or tablet. Needless to say between my phone, notebooks and tablets (I have been known to have as many as 5 of them in use at any given time.), there is lots of content.

Thus the impetus for this devotional. Instead of keeping it all to myself, I thought why not share some of what God has given me and perhaps it will encourage someone else! With my first book, *Fire New*, I was overwhelmed by the number of people who were encouraged by me simply sharing my testimony.

Countless numbers of people said it was like I was speaking directly to them or about a situation they were facing. From a 9-year-old little black boy to a 90-year-old white woman, the feedback was the same. It's funny how much we all have in common. And it's not until we begin to share our stories, fears, insecurities, etc., that we find out just how alike we truly are. So I decided to share some of my time with the Lord with you again in hopes that you will be inspired, motivated and encouraged to spend time in His presence. I pray that over the next 40 days, or whenever you read one of the passages, this devotional prompts you to have your own time with the lover of your soul.

Like the male birds in the early hours of dawn, He's calling you with His love song. Early in the morning, in the middle of the day, in the evening time He's singing to you. Trying to attract you to come spend time with Him in His presence, at His right hand where there are untold pleasures.

Let's Pray:

Heavenly Father, I stand in awe of you! In awe that you gave your only Son for me. In awe that you welcome me into your presence. Father, I thank you for the privilege of communing with you. Now Father, I ask that as I make time to read your word, along with this devotional, that you would continue to speak to me. I pray that each day you would bring me fresh insight into your word. I'm looking forward to our time together over the next 40 days and beyond. In Jesus' name, Amen.

A Call To Action:

What has God said to you about today's devotional?

What things can you do, or what steps can you take to apply today's devotional?

DAY 2:
PRACTICE MAKES...PEACE

(Key Passage: Philippians 4:1-9)

Put into practice what you learned and received from me, both from my words and from my actions. And the God who gives us peace will be with you."

Philippians 4:9 (Good News Translation)

NBA superstar Allen Iverson ("AI" as he was affectionately known), was once criticized for a press conference he did, during which he made comments that seemed to suggest he didn't care to or see the need to practice playing basketball. The media, fans and basketball pundits alike, without having the full context of the interview, trashed Iverson. But what they didn't know, see or hear was that Iverson's friend had recently died. And as Iverson was dealing with his own emotions around his friend's death, all the media seemed to be concerned about was his basketball practice. I too saw and heard the interview. But my take on it was a little different. I didn't think Iverson needed to be concerned about practice. He was the star of the Philadelphia 76ers (my hometown team). He scored lots of points, he always gave it 100 percent, and he was the toughest player on the court. So in my humble, non-sports-enthusiast opinion, he didn't need to practice—not as much as the rest of the players on the team did.

However when it comes to the things of God, practice is essential. Regardless of how long you've been saved, or how much of the Bible you know—practice is always a must. One of the reasons Apostle Paul wrote the Book of Philippians was to encourage believers how to stay joyful and peaceful. In the 4th chapter, he admonishes them to rejoice in the Lord always, and instead of worrying, pray about everything. Worrying is an ugly monster and a trick of the enemy. We worry about what we've done in the past even though we can't go back and change it. We worry about what we want to do in the future, even though we can't move time ahead, nor do we know whether we'll actually live to see the future. And all that worrying about the past and the future prohibits us from living in the present, the here and now. I read somewhere that less than ten percent of the things we worry about ever actually occur.

To help those of us who tend to worry a lot, Paul gives some practical advice. Understanding that our worrying comes from the things we think about, Paul encourages believers to turn off the "bad news station" and turn on the "good news station" in our minds. He says to "fill our minds with those things that are good and that deserve praise: things that are true, noble, right, pure, lovely, and honorable" (Philippians 4:8, GNT). And put the things that we've learned into practice.

If we could just train our minds to believe the best and not the worst. To believe what God says and not what society says. To believe the report of the Lord and not the doctor's report, God's peace would overwhelm us and worry would have no choice but to dissipate. But we've got to practice. Thinking pure and noble thoughts doesn't occur automatically. Our world is bombarded with bad news. In the midst of writing this devotional, we're facing the Covid-19 pandemic. All we hear on TV, radio and social media is the number of deaths occurring as a result of the virus. If we're not careful, all that bad news will cause us to wonder whether we have the virus if we make a simple cough. However practicing listening to the "good news station" will encourage and uplift our spirits. Some of the tunes you'll hear on the "good news station" are,

- I can do all things through Christ which gives me strength. (Philippians 4:13)
- Nothing can separate me from the love of God. (Romans 8:38)
- The Lord is my refuge and strength, a very present help in trouble. (Psalm 46:1); and one of my favorites,
- We are God's masterpiece created in Christ Jesus for good works. (Ephesians 2:10)

So practice, practice, practice. When negative, self-defeating thoughts come to your mind, and they will, tell yourself, and tell the devil too, "I have the mind of Christ," and that garbage can no longer occupy space in your mind. Paul says when we practice the things we've learned and seen and heard, God's peace will be with us. And His peace is far beyond human understanding and keeps us in union with Jesus Christ. While the saying, "Practice makes perfect" may not apply in our walk with God, practice makes peace sure does.

Let's Pray:

Dear God, thank you for your peace. The peace that you give calms all my fears. I pray that in times of worry, stress and anxiety you will remind me that when I pray instead of worrying, you promise to give me a peace that surpasses all understanding. Holy Spirit, teach me to set my mind on the promises of God and then to put on my helmet of salvation so that I won't forget what you said. As I meditate on your word and practice what it says, you promised to be with me, and when I have you, I have your peace. In Jesus' name, Amen.

A Call To Action:

What has God said to you about today's devotional?

What things can you do, or what steps can you take to apply today's devotional?

DAY 3:
THE MIDAS TOUCH

(Key Passage: Psalm 1:1-6)

"Oh, the joys of those who do not follow the advice of the wicked, or stand around with sinners, or join in with mockers. But they delight in the law of the LORD meditating on it day and night. They are like trees planted along the riverbank, bearing fruit each season. Their leaves never wither, and they prosper in all they do."

Psalm 1:1-3 (New Living Translation)

What does success look like to you? Money? Fame? Wisdom? Lots of friends? Abundant wealth? Success can mean different things to different people. I've come to understand that success to me is knowing God's will for my life and accomplishing it. Jesus was a great example of what success looks like. He came to earth in fleshly form for a purpose, on purpose and with purpose. And in approximately thirty-three short years, He accomplished all that He was sent to do. And when He died, He proclaimed, "It is finished" and went back to be with the Father. While He walked this earth, He left no stone unturned, no work undone, no task incomplete. Wow—that's major success right there. How many of us will be able to testify that when we leave this earth we will be satisfied that everything God purposed for us to do was done? I sure hope I'll have that testimony.

One of the things that hindered me from truly going after everything God had for me was fear. Fear of rejection, fear of failure, fear of what people would say, fear that I wasn't good enough. I had to really pray and ask the Lord to help me conquer and move past my fears. And once I started meditating on His word, day by day I started moving in purpose and intentionally leaving fear behind. It's amazing what God's word can do for you and me when we meditate on it. Meditate means to reflect on, to study, to ponder. I would read scriptures dealing with overcoming fear, write them on a post-it, stick it on my bathroom mirror, say them out loud each day. I would read them all throughout the day, telling myself over and over that God didn't give me a spirit of fear. And each day I would get stronger and stronger and more courageous.

What stops you from reaching for God's best for you? Is it fear for you too? What about your lack of education? Is it a criminal record or lack of finances? Whatever it is, I challenge you to go to the word of God and find scriptures that will encourage and motivate you to move beyond your circumstance and press into all that God has for you. The Book of Ephesians lets us know that the word of God is one of our spiritual weapons (Ephesians 6:17), referring to it as a sword. an offensive spiritual weapon; it puts our enemies on notice. We use the word of God to attack and slice through every lie that comes against the word of God (2 Corinthians 10:5).

Psalm 119 is the longest chapter in the Bible, and it's all about the word of God. The Psalmist talks about the promises in the word of God and how he delights in the word of God. He asks the Lord to teach him the word of God and he longs for the word of God. He proclaims that God's word is faithful and true and very pure. That Psalm is a true testament to how powerful the word of God is. We will never be let down when we meditate on the word of God. Success is inevitable for those who study God's word and live by it.

There is a tale in Greek mythology about a king named Midas, who after winning the favor of a god named Dionysus, was granted a wish for anything he desired. Midas wished that everything he touched would turn to gold. The wish was granted and at first it was wonderful—a gold chair, a gold door, a gold bathtub. But soon enough Midas' fortune turned tragic when he realized he would starve to death because when he touched his food, it too turned to gold. The legend goes on to say that Midas realized the error of his ways and asked that the wish be reversed, and he lived a happy life, being content with what he had.

For believers, there is no need to turn to Greek mythology or some dead Greek god to obtain success. For the Bible gives us instructions on how to prosper in everything we do. And we don't have to wish for it either. When we shun wickedness and instead take pleasure in meditating on God's word, we are promised success. Live life like it's golden.

Let's Pray:

Dear Lord, thank you for the success I have in you. Thank you that your word teaches me how to have true success that doesn't wither away. I don't have to cheat, scam or deceive my way to success. Instead meditating on your word day and night trains me to be successful in everything I do. Thank you for your promise that says the blessing of the Lord makes me rich, and adds no sorrow with it (Proverbs 10:22). In Jesus' name, Amen.

A Call To Action:

What has God said to you about today's devotional?

What things can you do, or what steps can you take to apply today's devotional?

DAY 4:
I KNOW WHO I AM

(Key Passage: Matthew 4:1-11)

"Now the tempter came to Him, he said, 'If You are the Son of God, command that these stones become bread." But He answered and said, "It is written, 'Man shall not live by bread alone, but by every word that proceeds from the mouth of God.'"

Matthew 4:3-4 (NKJV)

The first 11 verses of the 4th chapter of the Book of Matthew tell of an interaction between Jesus and Satan. Jesus has been in the wilderness, without food, on a fast for 40 days. So here comes Satan to try to take advantage of Jesus in His weakened physical state. Twice Satan says to Jesus, if You are the Son of God then do this or that. Satan was trying to tempt Jesus to "prove" Himself by doing something that was against God's will. But Jesus wouldn't fall for any of Satan's tricks even though He was physically weak. Because at all times Jesus knew exactly who He was. Satan tempted Jesus by trying to get Him to turn stones into bread, but Jesus knew He was the bread of life. Satan tempted Jesus by trying to get Him to throw Himself down to worship at Satan's feet, but Jesus knew He was the High

Priest, the Exalted One. Satan tried to tempt Jesus by offering Him the kingdoms of the world; but Jesus knew that the earth and everything in it were already His. Yes, Jesus knew who He was. After that Satan left Him alone.

Knowing who we are in God is so important to us becoming who God wants us to be. Understanding God's will for your life, knowing your purpose and being secure with the role you play guards against jealousy, envy and pride. When you know the plans that God has for your life, you won't need to prove yourself to anyone. Knowing who you are in God gives your life meaning, clarity and direction. You will have a laser-like focus on doing only those things that the Father tells you to do. Nothing more, nothing less. There's really nothing Satan can do to someone who knows who they are. Just like he left Jesus alone, he'll leave you alone, for the moment. But we've got to remain steadfast and unmovable; determined not to be anything other than who God created us to be. Being anything else would make us counterfeits.

I struggled with this for a very long time—not knowing who I was. I would try to be like other people who I thought had it all together. I would idolize gifts and abilities I saw in other people because I didn't understand the gifts that God instilled in me. I would try to "force" myself to fit into jobs, relationships, and even friendships all because I didn't know who I was, so I couldn't value what I brought to the table. It was a very confusing time for me. Trying all sorts of things, to no avail, because I didn't know what God had for me. But once I started seeking God for wisdom and guidance He opened my eyes. I'd pray like Paul prayed in Colossians 1, that I'd be filled with the knowledge of His will in all wisdom and spiritual understanding. I'd pray like Paul prayed in Ephesians 1, that the eyes of my understanding would be enlightened and that I would know the hope of His calling. The more I prayed, the more God opened my eyes. Until I no longer desired to be anyone other than who He made me to be.

There is something super special about every one of us, and Satan knows it. He wants to stop you from fulfilling God's plan for your life. But you have to remember that you are fearfully and wonderfully made (Psalm 139:14). God has a great plan for our lives and if we're going to accomplish great things, we must be secure with who He made us to be. Ask your Heavenly Father to show you just who He made you to be. Ask Him to reveal to you what gifts, talents and abilities He's placed inside you. God's desire is for His children to know that we are secure in Him. Colossians 2:10 says we are complete in Him (Christ) who is head of all. Complete means we are whole, lacking absolutely nothing. We don't have to prove to anyone that we are qualified, equipped, or capable. Christ makes us qualified, Christ makes us equipped, Christ makes us capable. We can do *ALL* things through Christ who gives us strength (Philippians 4:13).

I encourage you to meditate on scriptures that tell of who you are in God. Read Ephesians 2:10 (New Living Translation), "For we are God's masterpiece. He has created us anew in Christ Jesus, so we can do the good things he planned for us long ago." Read 1 Peter 2:9 (NLT), "But you are not like that, for you are a chosen people. You are royal priests, a holy nation, God's very own possession. As a result, you can show others the goodness of God, for he called you out of the darkness into his wonderful light." Read John 15:15 (New American Standard Bible), "No longer do I call you servants, for a servant does not know what his master is doing; but I have called you friends, for all things that I heard from My Father I have made known to you."

It's when we begin to have an appreciation for just how awesome we are in God that we'll understand our worth. Then no one, not even Satan, can convince us to be anything other than who God created us to be. I now know who I am. Do you?

Let's Pray:

Lord God, thank you that you created me on purpose, with purpose and for purpose. Thank you that I am complete in you and You supply everything I need for life and godliness. I am no longer a servant to other people's opinions of me, I no longer do things to try to fit in. I know you have a special place and purpose for me, and when I follow your voice, you lead me in paths of righteousness. In Jesus' name, Amen.

A Call To Action:

What has God said to you about today's devotional?

What things can you do, or what steps can you take to apply today's devotional?

DAY 5:

USE WHAT YOU GOT TO GET WHAT YOU WANT

(Key Passage: 2 Kings 4:1-7)

"Elisha said to her, 'What shall I do for you? Tell me, what do have [of value] in the house?'"

2 Kings 4:2 (Amplified Bible)

The Beverly Hillbillies is an old TV sitcom that I used to watch. It was about a poor "backwoods" family from the Ozarks of Arkansas who discovered oil on their land, so they moved to Beverly Hills, California. I'm sure you can imagine what the superficial swanky neighbors in Beverly Hills thought of their new unsophisticated neighbors. The show's theme song was played on a banjo and was about a poor man named Jeb who barely made enough to keep his family fed. One day he was hunting for some food, shot a hole in the ground, and oil came shooting up from the ground. That made for some great TV back in the day, LOL. That show was my first introduction into the oil business. It was because of that show that I understood that oil was big business. The petroleum (oil) has been utilized by humans for over 5,000 years.

In biblical times there was another family that was in the oil business, a woman and her two sons. The Bible doesn't give their names, it only states that her husband had died and creditors were coming to take her two sons away as slaves, as repayment for outstanding debt the family owed. This woman and her two sons were in a desperate situation. So she went to the prophet of God, Elisha, and told him what was going on. Elisha asked her what she wanted him to do about it, since he didn't have the money. Then he asked her what she had of value at home. Her reply? She had nothing but a jar of oil. Elisha then told her to go and borrow as many empty containers as she could from her neighbors—lots of them. He said for her and her sons to then go in the house, close the door and start pouring the oil that she had in the containers. When she started pouring the oil from the jar she had into the jars she'd borrowed a miracle started happening. She was able to fill all of the containers she borrowed with oil. The oil didn't stop flowing out until all the containers were filled. Then Elisha told her to sell the oil, repay her debt and live off the rest. Wow.

There's a whole lot of content packed into these seven verses, but I'll focus on two things for today. One, you already have within you what you need to be successful. 2 Peter 1:3 (NKJV) says, "As His divine power has given to us all things that pertain to life and godliness, through the knowledge of Him who called us by glory and virtue." This scripture lets us know that God has already given us everything we need. Don't discount who you are or what you have. Look deep within yourself, there is something there of value. You already have what you need for your own miracle. You have the peace you need, you have the courage you need, you have the connections you need. It's already there. That woman said she had nothing except a jar of oil. She discounted what God could do with a little jar of oil. Her response should have been that she had a jar of oil, period. Even though she didn't value what she had, she was obedient to the prophet's command and did as he said. When she moved in obedience, she was able to see the miracle-working power of God. But not only did she see it, her children saw it. Allow your obedience to God to be a testimony to your family also.

The second thing I want to highlight from this power packed story is that the miracle wasn't complete just because she filled the containers with oil. That was only part of the process. If she had stopped at this point, she would have had a house full of oil and still had debt that needed to be repaid. The next step was to sell the oil. Sometimes we can get so excited about what God is doing in our lives that we stop before He's completely done blessing us. I want to caution you (and myself.) to follow through on *all* of God's instructions. It was only after she sold the jars of oil that she was able to get the money to repay the creditors. She made so much money that after repaying her debt, she and her sons were able to live off the rest. Here again, she got her children involved. They had a front row seat to witness the blessing of obedience and the power of God. And if

I can sneak in a third point, it would be to allow your children to get involved in the work of the Lord. If they see you struggling, worried and afraid. Then let them also see you praying, reading and giving. And when your situation turns around, they'll know that it was because mom, dad, auntie, uncle, grandmom or granddad was faithful to God and did just what He said.

Let's Pray:

Dear God, thank you for giving me everything I need. Thank you for blessing my little and making it much. Help me to see the value that you've placed inside of me. I want my children to see and know that we serve an awesome God. Help me to be an example to them of what it means to be an obedient child so that they will see your power and your goodness. In Jesus' name, Amen.

A Call To Action:

What has God said to you about today's devotional?

____

____

____

____

____

____

____

____

What things can you do, or what steps can you take to apply today's devotional?

____

____

____

____

____

____

____

____

____

DAY 6:
FRIENDS WITH BENEFITS

(Key Passage: Psalm 103:1-22)

"I no longer call you servants, because a servant does not know his master's business. Instead, I have called you friends, for everything that I learned from my Father I have made known to you."

John 15:15 (New International Version)

"Bless the LORD, O my soul, and forget not all His benefits."

Psalm 103:2 (NKJV)

When our son started working at Amazon, like many other companies, they sent home a package explaining that one of the benefits offered to employees was the opportunity to contribute to a deferred compensation plan. This is where they withhold a certain amount or percentage of your wages to put into a retirement account. Me being a CPA, I was able to explain the pros and cons of the different options within the plan and the tax advantages of each option. The one thing I really liked about their plan was that it was an automatic enrollment plan. So if a new employee failed to choose how much they wanted to contribute to the plan, Amazon would automatically enroll that employee in the plan after 90 days at a certain percentage of their wages. I believe that's a great way to get new employees, particularly younger employees, to start saving for retirement without it taking any effort on their part.

Like Amazon, when we become Christians, we are automatically enrolled in God's benefits package. His benefits package offers abundantly more than just saving for retirement. In fact it includes benefits for all of eternity. Jesus said in John 15:15 that we are no longer servants, we are His friends. And the Bible provides countless promises and benefits for those of us who are friends of God.

It's widely believed that King David wrote Psalm 103. In it he lists some of the great benefits we receive from God. The Psalmist starts off by encouraging himself (and us) to bless the Lord with everything that's in us—our whole hearts, our entire being. He then says we ought to bless the Lord, and while we're blessing Him, don't forget about all of the benefits He bestows upon us. He then goes on to list some of the reasons why he (and we) should bless the Lord. This list goes on and on, but I'll list just a few here:

- He forgives all our iniquities. Let me say right here that if God didn't provide this, the benefit of forgiveness of our sins, then we would be lost and without any hope. I heard one pastor put it this way, "If you can't get excited about your sins being forgiven, you might not really be saved." He was joking, but not really. As Christians we must be aware that the forgiveness of our sins is key to us having a relationship with God.

- He heals all our diseases. Ultimately God is our healer. Not the doctors, not the medicine. It's God alone who has the power to heal.
- He redeems our lives from destruction. God saves our lives from death and separation from Him. He provided Jesus as our kinsman redeemer, to deliver us from the destruction of hell. In the Old Testament if you couldn't afford to pay a debt you owed you would have to sell all of your property or sell yourself into slavery. But a relative could step up and pay the debt for you and redeem you from losing everything you owned, including your freedom. That's what Jesus did for us when He died on the cross; He paid our debt for sin and now we are redeemed.
- He crowns us with love and mercy. Our lives are covered in God's love and mercy for us. We wear them like a king or queen wears a crown. God's love and mercy are what make us royalty.

These are just a few of the gems contained in God's benefits package. If you read Psalm 103 in its entirety, you'll find more benefits that David recalls to his mind. I encourage you, spend some time learning about all the benefits of being a friend of God. Just like when you start a new job, you learn about all the benefits so that you can take advantage of them: medical, dental, vacation days, sick days, retirement, etc. We should do the same with God's benefits package. Think about all of the things God has done, is doing, and will continue to do for us. I believe you'll be like David and shout, "Bless the Lord O my soul."

Let's Pray:

Dear God, thank you for being my friend. Thank you for providing me with the greatest benefits package. You provided forgiveness of my sins, healing of my diseases, love, mercy, salvation and so much more. God, without your benefits I'd be lost like a ship without a sail. But because you call me friend, you provide for me like no one else. I love you, Lord, and I will bless you with all my heart. In Jesus' name, Amen.

A Call To Action:

What has God said to you about today's devotional?

What things can you do, or what steps can you take to apply today's devotional?

DAY 7:
NOT PERFECT, BUT EXCELLENT

(Key Passage: Philippians 3:12-21)

"I don't mean to say I am perfect. I haven't learned all I should even yet, but I keep working toward that day when I will finally be all that Christ saved me for and wants me to be. No, dear brothers, I am still not all I should be, but I am bringing all my energies to bear on this one thing: Forgetting the past and looking forward to what lies ahead, I strain to reach the end of the race and receive the prize for which God is calling us up to heaven because of what Christ Jesus did for us."

Philippians 3:12-14 (Living Bible)

I sometimes can be a bit of a perfectionist. When I'm that way, my perfectionism causes me to focus on the minutia instead of the bigger picture; it's kind of like not seeing the forest for the trees. I've learned that perfectionism can be a form of pride—ouch. So when I'm prideful and full of myself, the spotlight turns into a heat lamp and I sweat big time. I'm constantly reminding myself that it's not about me being perfect, it's about God shining through me, using me to bring

Him glory. It's no fun trying to be perfect, never making a mistake. Perfection focuses on doing the thing exactly right, while excellence focuses on doing the right thing. I'd rather shoot for excellence and let the chips fall where they may.

There were some Pharisees in the Bible who were always trying to catch Jesus doing something against Jewish law. They were the "perfectionists" of the law. There's a story in the Book of Mark, the 3rd chapter, that tells of a time on the Sabbath day when a man with a disfigured hand was in the synagogue where Jesus was. The Pharisees stood by secretly watching to see whether Jesus would heal the man as it was against Jewish law to do any work on the Sabbath day, apparently, including healing. So Jesus asked them, "Is it all right to do kind deeds on Sabbath days? Or is this a day for doing harm?" The Pharisees didn't answer Him. The Bible says Jesus was angry at the hardness of their hearts. He turned to the man with the disfigured hand and told him to stretch out his hand. And when he did, his hand was healed and restored. That story is an example of doing things right versus doing the right thing. Isaiah 29:13 (NIV) states, "The Lord says: "These people come near to me with their mouth and honor me with their lips, but their hearts are far from me. Their worship of me is based on merely human rules they have been taught."

I'm so glad God does not require our perfection. My love for Him drives me to do things with a spirit of excellence, according to Colossians 3:23 but never perfection. And who is perfect anyway? No one but God. As long as we strive to do the best we can with what we know and have, we're on the right track.

My husband and I were on a cruise a few years ago. They had a 3-on-3 basketball tournament and some of the "older" men on the ship were playing against each other. Now my husband used to be a great basketball player in high school, but some thirty years later—not so much. These guys were missing shots, slow, tripping over themselves, panting and out of breath—it was like watching the game in slow motion. However some of the other wives and I dutifully sat by and cheered them on. In the end my husband's team won. He was so hyped, talking trash and fist bumping. Well I don't think he so much as said the word basketball the remainder of the cruise. His body told on him and it was not a pretty story. My point is, those guys fought and won the game, no matter how old, tired and out of sync they were. They fought hard. It wasn't a pretty win, but it was a win nonetheless. It wasn't a perfect win, but their excellence won the game—and the Royal Caribbean gold medal, LOL.

Paul said in Philippians 3:13-14, listen brothers (and sisters) I'm not perfect and I'm not all that I should be. But because I have a spirit of excellence I keep going, I keep pushing. Forgetting about what's in the past, I look forward to everything that God has ahead of me. Paul was determined to get there. He had to go through being shipwrecked, whipped, jailed and mocked. But when he came to the end of his life, he was able to testify, "I have fought a good fight, I have finished my course, I have kept the faith" (2 Timothy 4:7). Like Paul, we won't always have an easy time and we won't always get it right. But if we stay focused on Jesus and keep pushing forward, we will receive our prize. We may not be able to attain perfection, but we can all strive to do things in excellence.

Let's Pray:

Father God, it is such a relief that you don't require me to be perfect. Thank you because you make up for all of my weaknesses and shortcomings. True perfection comes from knowing you and doing Your will. Help me to have an excellent spirit in everything I do. Help me not to dwell on past mistakes, but to press forward until I reach the prize of your high calling in Christ. In Jesus' name, Amen.

A Call To Action:

What has God said to you about today's devotional?

What things can you do, or what steps can you take to apply today's devotional?

DAY 8:
STAY IN THE RACE

(Key Passage: 1 Thessalonians 5:12-19)

"Rejoice always, pray without ceasing,
in everything give thanks; for this is the will of God
in Christ Jesus for you."

1 Thessalonians 5:16-18 (NKJV)

Years ago I tried to get into running. Black Girls Run had me all excited and I was going to join them and run a 5k race. I came across a program (I believe it was one of theirs) that was supposed to help me move from the couch to running a 5k. It started with a brisk walk, and then a walk with intermittent running. You'd then move to more running than walking and eventually to a full run for 5 kilometers. Sounds great, right? Well, it lasted all of two weeks for me. I never got past the walk with intermittent running. I've come to realize that I just don't like running. But I love watching track and field on television or even in person. I admire people who can distance run. In Philadelphia, where I'm from, there's a race called the Broad Street Run which is about 10 miles. I have several family members and friends who participate in that run. From my couch I pray for them and cheer them on, LOL. But for some reason I just can't get into running. I can do a lot of walking though. I just don't think I have the endurance it takes for running.

The Bible refers to our Christian walk as being like running a race. Hebrews 12:1, Galatians 5:7, and Philippians 2:16 all refer to us running with patience, running well and not running in vain. In order for us to stay in the Christian race and press toward the mark (as Paul urges in Philippians 3:14), we need spiritual endurance. The Merriam-Webster online dictionary defines endurance as the ability to withstand hardship or adversity. The Bible tells us that we will suffer persecution and we will have trials, so we need to know something about how to endure. That's what Paul was trying to do for the church in Thessalonica—help them endure hard times. In doing so, he wrote 1 and 2 Thessalonians to encourage them. But in 1 Thessalonians Paul tells them three simple but key phrases that I believe will go a long way in helping us all maintain our spiritual endurance. One, rejoice always; two, pray without ceasing and three, in everything give thanks.

Rejoice means to *re*new your *joy.* It has to be done over and over again by letting the joy of the Lord be your strength (Nehemiah 8:10). Joy is different from happiness in that happiness is based on your outward circumstances. But joy, real joy, is an internal peace that comes from knowing you are a child of God.

Pray without ceasing means don't stop. You can pray anywhere, anytime, and about anything. Open your mouth and talk to God. You have His undivided attention in prayer. Never stop talking to God about your hopes and dreams. Your ups and downs. Your worries and frustrations. He delights to hear from you. He's waiting to help you. Take it to Him in prayer.

In everything give thanks means to be thankful at all times. We don't have to be thankful for everything, especially things like sickness, job loss or losing a loved one. But we can still be thankful in everything. There's something special about thanksgiving. It shows God how grateful we are when we're full of thanks. Helen Keller was a famous teacher, author and advocate. She was born a perfectly healthy baby until about 19 months old when she contracted scarlet fever, leaving her deaf and blind. In dealing with her dark and noiseless life, she became angry and violent, often throwing things. At age 7 her parents sought out a tutor for Helen and engaged the services of Anne Sullivan who worked tirelessly with Helen. With Anne's help, Helen was able to reach unbelievable heights. She learned sign language, how to spell, how to communicate with others and to read braille. Helen then went on to graduate college, became a professor, became an author and traveled as an advocate for the deaf and blind. What's even more remarkable about Helen is that she was introduced to God and she said this of her life, "For three things I thank God every day of my life: Thanks that He gave me knowledge of His word, deep thanks that He set in my darkness the light of faith; and deepest thanks that I have another life to look forward to, a life of joyous light and flowers and heavenly song." Now surely if Helen Keller could thank God in her dark, silent world, you and I can find something to thank God for.

So be encouraged. Stay in the race and don't give up. Build up your spiritual endurance by rejoicing always, praying without ceasing and giving thanks in everything—for this is the will of God in Christ Jesus concerning you.

Let's Pray:

Thank you, Lord; thank you, Lord; thank you, Lord for all you've done for me. I now realize that if I want to build up my endurance to stay in this Christian race, I've got to rejoice, pray and give thanks. Today I make a commitment to do those three things every day. In Jesus' name, Amen.

A Call To Action:

What has God said to you about today's devotional?

What things can you do, or what steps can you take to apply today's devotional?

DAY 9:
NOW I GET IT

(Key Passage: Genesis 37:1-36)

"You intended to harm me, but God intended it all for good. He brought me to this position so I could save the lives of many people."

Genesis 50:20 (NLT)

The saying hindsight is 20/20 never rang more true than for Joseph. The saying means that we don't truly see things clearly until after we've come through them and can look back to really see what happened. Have you ever gone through something and asked yourself, or God, what was it all for? I don't understand why I'm in this situation. But then weeks, months or years later, you get a revelation of how that former experience prepared you for something you're currently dealing with. When we're going through a tough time, we can get so consumed by our pain, heartache, or our mistreatment by others that we don't see the bigger picture, or the good that can come from our tough situation.

I'm sure Joseph must have felt like that a time or two—or twelve. Joseph was a dreamer and he wasn't shy about telling people his dreams, especially his brothers. He told them of a dream he had where he ruled over them and they served him. Imagine their indignation. We're going to serve you, our younger brother? I'm sure they laughed at Joseph. Now Joseph's father loved him very much and treated him with favor. Because his older brothers were jealous of him, they sold him to some foreigners who made him a slave. Because the Lord was with him, Joseph was promoted to being the personal assistant of a high ranking official in Egypt. Then he was falsely accused of raping the official's wife, so he went to prison. Have you ever been there? One tragedy happens, and just as you're getting over it, something else happens that seems to set you back again. I've been there. Years went by and while Joseph was serving his prison sentence, he interpreted a dream for the king of Egypt, which caused him to win the favor of the king. Then Joseph was released from prison and appointed second in command of all of Egypt. You have to read the full story in Genesis chapters 37 through 50 to get all the juicy details.

In Genesis chapter 50, Joseph comes to his hindsight 20/20 moment. You see what happened was Joseph's brothers ended up having to come to Egypt, to Joseph, to buy food to survive a famine. With Joseph being the second in command, he was over the food distribution, so if anyone wanted food, they had to come through Joseph. His brothers had no idea that the young boy they sold into slavery all those years ago had now become the second most powerful man in Egypt. And when Joseph revealed himself to his brothers, they were scared for their lives. But Joseph, he wept for joy. You see Joseph knew something about God that you and I can learn today. God doesn't make any mistakes. And regardless of the circumstances in our lives, God can get something good out of them. Joseph told his brothers (I'm paraphrasing), "Don't be afraid. Because although you meant it for evil, I had to go through everything I went through, because God wanted me in this position, so that many lives would be saved." If his brothers hadn't sold him to those traveling foreigners, Joseph would not have been in Egypt. While Joseph was in Egypt and when he was in prison, Joseph was learning valuable life skills. He learned humility, patience, communication skills, and how to be a good worker. God was building Joseph's character while simultaneously setting the stage for Joseph's comeback.

The Bible takes care to mention that with each tragedy Joseph went through, God was still with him. It mentions several times that God gave Joseph favor. Favor with Potiphar. Favor with the prison guards. And eventually favor with the king of Egypt. Joseph didn't let his circumstances get him down. He didn't allow his hardships to sour his attitude about life. And because of it, when God decided it was Joseph's time, everyone felt that Joseph was qualified for the job.

Remember our attitude matters. If you're in a tough time right now, don't let it sour you. Know that God is still with you and working in your situation. He will bring you out at His appointed time, and you'll look back, like Joseph, and declare, "I thought it was for my harm, but God turned it around for my good."

Let's Pray:

Dear Lord, thank you turning things around. Thank you for being with me even in my "prison" moments. Help me to keep a cheerful attitude while going through. Help me not to get weary in well doing. Keep me in your loving care until you decide to bring me out. I'll look back and realize that you were there all the time, and I'll give you all the glory. In Jesus' name, Amen.

A Call To Action:

What has God said to you about today's devotional?

What things can you do, or what steps can you take to apply today's devotional?

DAY 10:
I AM AND I WILL

(Key Passage: Isaiah 41:1-10)

"Fear not, for I am with you; be not dismayed, for I am your God. I will strengthen you, yes, I will help you, I will uphold you with My righteous right hand."

Isaiah 41:10 (NKJV)

I am a very task-oriented person. I like to do; I like helping people by doing for them; I enjoy finding solutions to problems. Whenever I'm not busy doing something, I have the tendency to feel unproductive or lazy. And when I have a problem to solve, my first intuition is to figure out a solution. At times I can rush ahead to problem-solving mode, or doing mode without considering how it will affect the people involved. In my angst to hurry and check that issue off the list, I can sometimes miss the deeper issue, the problem behind the problem. So one area of improvement for me in my walk with God is to allow Him to come up with the solutions to problems. Allow Him to direct me in what I should do.

Isaiah 41:10 has been a great scripture to help me to let go and let God be God. In this one verse, God gives two "I am" statements and three "I will" statements. In the first twenty verses of chapter 41, we are assured of God's help in our lives. First God says I am with you, so you don't have to fear. Sometimes we fear that if we don't jump right in and do something, then everything will fall apart. Or if we don't help solve a problem as soon as it occurs, then the bottom will fall out. But when we have those hurried responses, often we're operating out of fear. And God reminds us that He is with us. He knows the issues, He understands the challenge, and ultimately, He will help us figure out a solution. Second God says, "I am your God so don't be dismayed (or don't panic)." We must remember that God is our God. Fear is not our God. The problem is not our God. And even the people we may be trying to help are not our God. God is. And since He's our God, we should look to Him first before we start doing anything. So we don't have to be afraid, and we don't have to panic because God is with us and He's our God.

The three "I will" statements that God makes are I will strengthen you, I will help you and I will uphold you. I sometimes forget and need to be reminded, that anything I accomplish is done with God's strength and not my own. I can get so busy doing things simply because I know how to do them. But God will remind me that He gives me the strength to do everything. And also, when there are things that I'm afraid of doing, God reminds me that I can have confidence because I'm not relying on my own strength, but His strength. The Bible says in Zechariah 4:6 that it's not by (*your*) might, nor by (*your)* power, but it's by My spirit, says the Lord. (Emphasis mine). So much more can be accomplished when we rely on His strength and not our own. He has the best solution and He knows the best way to go. He understands all the people who will be affected and all the nuances of the situation that may be hidden from us. God says He will help us and He will uphold (sustain) us through it all.

Remember in trying to figure out solutions to life's problems (whether your own or in trying to help someone else), allow God to be the *I am* and *I will.* He is with us and He is our God. He will strengthen us, He will help us and He will uphold us. We are not left to ourselves to solve every issue or every crisis. Every issue doesn't have to be addressed right away. It's okay to wait on the Lord to direct us. And it's okay if we don't have an answer. That's when God will step in and show us just how God He really is. Don't fear, don't panic because God Is and God Will.

Let's Pray:

Dear Lord, thank you for being the source of my strength and the strength of my life. In those moments when I feel hurried to do something, help me to remember to look to you as my helper, my sustainer and my God. Holy Spirit, teach me to be confident in God's strength and not my own. And to allow Him to guide me through life's decisions. In Jesus' name, Amen.

A Call To Action:

What has God said to you about today's devotional?

What things can you do, or what steps can you take to apply today's devotional?

DAY 11:
RUN, TELL, SHARE

(Key Passage: 2 Kings 7:1-20)

"Finally, they said to each other, 'This is not right. This is a day of good news, and we aren't sharing it with anyone!. If we wait until morning, some calamity will certainly fall upon us. Come on, let's go back and tell the people at the palace.'"

2 Kings 7:9 (NLT)

There's a saying that good news travels fast, and bad news even faster. That expression rings so true, particularly when I look at the news. There are hardly any good stories to report. They seem to cram every story about the worst of our society into two hours of news reporting. That's so sad. That's why I don't watch the news very often. I know I need to stay informed of what's going on, but after hearing the story once, I'm done. Where are the positive, uplifting stories? The stories about the kindness and compassion for humanity? The stories of triumph and unexpected blessings. Those are the stories I like reading and hearing about. That's one of the reasons why I turn to the Bible to find stories like the one from which our verse today was taken.

The books of 1 and 2 Kings are fascinating books chronicling the reigns of several kings of Israel, spanning a period of about 400 years. In particular in 2 Kings where we get today's scripture, King Jehoram's idolatry (leading the people to fall into idolatry as well) caused the nation to be at odds with God. Because of this there was a severe famine in the city. So severe, in fact, that people would pay exorbitant prices to eat things they didn't ordinarily eat, like donkey's head and dove dung. People even resorted to eating their own children the famine was so bad. When Jehoram saw how badly the famine impacted the city, he was angry with God and with God's prophet, Elisha. Jehoram sent messengers to Elisha to let him know just how upset the king was. Elisha gave the king's messengers a word from the Lord and said, "By this time tomorrow in the markets of Samaria, six quarts of choice flour will cost only one piece of silver, and twelve quarts of barley grain will cost only one piece of silver." Indicating that the famine would be reversed and that choice foods would cost almost nothing.

Well the next day four men with leprosy were sitting outside the city. They were on the outside because those with leprosy were forbidden to come in close contact with anyone else. They were outcasts from society due to their skin condition. Apparently they were close to the end of their lives, which led them to ask themselves, *Why are we sitting here outside the city just waiting to die?* They reasoned that if they stayed outside the city they'd starve to death, and if they went into the city they'd be killed for coming in contact with other people. Either way, they'd die. They decided to take their chances on going into the city, and if they were caught, they would surrender to the king's army and plead for their lives.

As the lepers were walking towards the city, the Lord caused the king's army to hear the clatter of speeding horses and chariots like the sound of a great army approaching. The army got so spooked by the sound that they thought the surrounding nations were coming to attack them. So the king's army abandoned everything they had—food, clothing, shelter, horses, jewels—and fled for their lives. The lepers entered the city expecting to be besieged by the army, and instead had access to all the fleeing army's goods. They ate and drank and shouted and danced. Can you imagine? What they thought would be their death turned out to be their biggest blessing. And while they were celebrating, something hit them. They said this isn't right. We're here freely eating and drinking and everyone else is suffering in a famine. We've gotta go back and tell them about our good fortune. So that's what they did. And others were able to enjoy the good fortune as well.

This story is a reminder for you and me to share and tell of the good things God does for us. Instead of being quick to run and spread gossip, tell how the Lord woke you up this morning in your right mind. Instead of being eager to tell how badly they're treating you at the job, share how God makes sure you have food to eat each day. Instead of whispering down the lane about who's doing what with whom, share how Jesus died for you and saved you from a life of sin. Yes, tell of the goodness of the Lord. Now run, tell, share that.

Let's Pray:

Thank you, Father for every good and perfect gift that you give (James 1:17). Thank you for all the blessings I sometimes take for granted, like good health, food to eat and clothes to wear. Holy Spirit, prompt me when to share and tell of the great things that God has done for me. Let me never forget the greatest gift, salvation through Jesus Christ. I'll share that news with the world. In Jesus' name, Amen.

A Call To Action:

What has God said to you about today's devotional?

____
____
____
____
____
____
____
____

What things can you do, or what steps can you take to apply today's devotional?

____
____
____
____
____
____
____
____
____

DAY 12:
FEELINGS, FACTS AND FAITH

(Key Passage: Romans 1:8-17)

"For in it the righteousness of God is revealed from faith to faith; as it is written, 'The just shall live by faith.'"

Romans 1:17 (NKJV)

I'm a CPA by trade, so I typically deal with numbers in some shape or form for most of the day. I suppose I was drawn to accounting because of my need to have things orderly and logical. Or perhaps, as a result of being an accountant, I've developed a liking to have things orderly and logical. At any rate accounting and numbers make sense to me. There is typically no gray area, two plus two always equals four. Numbers are concrete, definite, firm. That's the way my mind works; that's how I process information. Very factual, logical and sequential.

My husband, on the other hand, is a feelings type of guy. He processes most things through the lens of how it makes him feel. He's sensitive and in touch with his emotions. He often will ask me how I feel about a certain situation, and a lot of times, I honestly don't feel anything. It makes the communications in our household very interesting at times. For me feelings are too "wishy-washy." Sometimes I feel good and sometimes I feel bad. One day I'm happy, another day I'm melancholy. There's nothing concrete, factual or sequential about feelings. I guess that's why I have such a hard time getting in touch with mine.

But whether you're a factual person like me, or you're more of a feelings person like my husband, there's something that overrides our feelings and the facts—our faith. Our faith supersedes our feelings, facts, fears and frustrations. Faith is the only way that believers are supposed to live. In times of lack or times of plenty. In times of sickness or times of health. In times of joy or times of sorrow—faith says that life is still worth living. When the facts suggest that I should be concerned about a doctor's report, my faith says by His stripes I'm healed (Isaiah 53:5). When the facts say that the layoff will deplete our finances, my faith says God supplies all my need according to His riches in glory (Philippians 4:19). When the facts say that my loved one has died and I should be overcome with grief, my faith says the joy of the Lord is my strength (Nehemiah 8:10).

At times we have to work hard at replacing our feelings, facts or both with faith. The scripture tells us our faith is based on things unseen. We can't see it, touch it, taste it or smell it...but somehow we know it exists. No wonder the Bible says we can't even begin to please God without faith because it takes faith just to believe that God exists. As we continue to grow in

Him, He will put us in more and more situations that will give our faith an opportunity to grow. Our journey may start out with something small like believing God for a good grade on an exam. And next you're having faith for the promotion on your job even though you're not the most qualified. Then you move to having faith for total healing of your body when the doctors don't even know what's wrong with you. Yes, our faith walk (notice, it's a walk and not a run) is slow and steady, gradually increasing with each situation we look to God for instead of ourselves. Pretty soon we are living by faith and it's an exciting adventure when we let go and let God drive.

God wants to fill our lives with so much joy and abundance. Not only an abundance of things, but an abundance of experiences with Him. Experiences where He has an opportunity to show off on our behalf. Proving Himself as God. If we're always relying on our feelings to determine what our day will be like, or if we're always looking to the facts to see how things will work out, we will miss those "God moments" when He surprises us with just how much He can do. The Passion Translation of Ephesians 3:20 puts it this way, "Never doubt God's mighty power to work in you and accomplish all this. He will achieve infinitely more than your greatest request, your most unbelievable dream, and exceed your wildest imagination. He will outdo them all, for His miraculous power constantly energizes you." This is why the just live life by faith.

Let's Pray:

God, I'm sorry for the times when I've allowed my feelings and the facts to get the best of me, replacing my faith in you with fear. God, I know that you don't give us a fearful spirit, so today I choose to strengthen my faith. Holy Spirit, remind me not to lean on my own understanding, but to acknowledge God in all of my ways (Proverbs 3:5-6). Thank you that with a little faith, I can accomplish much. I choose to trust you, Lord. In Jesus' name, Amen.

A Call To Action:

What has God said to you about today's devotional?

What things can you do, or what steps can you take to apply today's devotional?

DAY 13:
DON'T BE A COPYCAT

(Key Passage: Romans 12:1-21)

"Don't copy the behavior and customs of this world, but let God transform you into a new person by changing the way you think. Then you will learn to know God's will for you, which is good and pleasing and perfect."

Romans 12:2 (NLT)

I watched the movie *Catch Me If You Can* by Steven Spielberg at least three times in totality. I've watched pieces of it many more times. It's a crime movie based on the life of Frank Abagnale who was a wildly successful con artist, performing cons that amassed millions of dollars. One of his crimes was check fraud. He became so successful at it that the FBI turned to him to help catch other check forgers. Forgery involves the skill of copying a document, signature or banknote so that it passes as an original. The person in possession of the originals don't need a forgery because they have the real thing. That's what today's scripture reminds us of.

When we become born again Christians, 2 Corinthians 5:17 tells us that old things are passed away and all things become new. When Nicodemus came to Jesus in the 3rd chapter of the Book of John, Jesus told him that he must be born again to enter the kingdom of God. The same applies to you and me. And the way that we begin to become born again so that all things can become new is by doing what Romans 12:2 says. When we are children, we are taught all kinds of things by our parents, teachers, friends and society at large. Some of the things we're taught are good: how to tie our shoes, how to say our alphabet, how to ride a bike, or even fix a leaky faucet. Other times we may have been taught some not so good things: if someone hits you, hit them back; it's okay to tell a "little white lie," do whatever it takes to get as much money as you can, etc. And if you were never taught any of the things I mentioned, the fact that we are all sinners saved by God's grace suggests that every one of us has been taught or learned something that goes against God's nature.

Because of this we have to allow God to transform us and change us into who He desires us to be. We cannot bring the behaviors and customs of our old way of thinking into our new lives in God's kingdom. In other words we cannot copy or forge the world's views into God's kingdom. His kingdom is run by a different set of rules and our old mindset won't serve us well. It can be tough in the beginning—this new way of thinking—but the more we practice and read God's word, the less difficult it becomes. And soon enough you'll learn to pray for the person who cursed you out, or you'll learn to forgive your enemies, even if they haven't said they are sorry.

When we let go of being a copycat of the world's views, and embrace the new thinking God wants us to have, then we learn God's will for our lives. We won't be God's original masterpiece if we're trying to be a forgery of the world. Let that go. What God has for us is so much better than what the world could offer. Romans 12:1 (TPT) says, "Beloved friends, what should be our proper response to God's marvelous mercies? I encourage you to surrender yourselves to God to be his sacred, living sacrifices. And live in holiness, experiencing all that delights his heart. For this becomes your genuine expression of worship." We worship God by surrendering to Him and allowing Him to transform us into a new creation. That way we'll receive His good, pleasing and perfect will for our lives. Why be a copycat when you were created to be an original.

Let's Pray:

Father God, my creator, thank you for bringing me out of darkness into your marvelous light. Thank you for making me into a beautiful masterpiece of your choosing. When I begin to look at the world and I start to desire their ways, Holy Spirit, help me to surrender my body to God and let Him transform me. I want to do those things that please you, Lord. So help me to meditate on your word so that you can make me new. In Jesus' name, Amen.

A Call To Action:

What has God said to you about today's devotional?

____

What things can you do, or what steps can you take to apply today's devotional?

____

DAY 14:
I AM LOVED...I AM CHOSEN

(Key Passage: Genesis 29:15-35)

"When the LORD saw that Leah was unloved, He opened her womb; but Rachel was barren."

Genesis 29:31 (NKJV)

Some experts agree that one of the basic needs all humans have is the need to be loved and accepted. I suspect this need drives more of our decision-making than some of us care to admit, or more than we even realize. It's why so many of us try so hard to please other people. Without realizing it, we say "Yes" to things we really don't want to do. We take fifty pictures just to post on social media the one that makes us look the best. We stay in that relationship longer than we should because we don't want to be the person at the BBQ without a mate. Yes our need to be loved and accepted by others will have us doing things we normally wouldn't do. And we'll do anything just so that we aren't perceived as being the "bad guy."

There are times when all of our people-pleasing amounts to nothing. That person still doesn't like us. We still didn't get the promotion. We still didn't get an invite to join the club. It's a defeating feeling when we try so hard to be liked and come up short. Ask me how I know. Been there, done that, and can write the book...well, at least today's topic. The 29th chapter of Genesis recounts the story of a woman named Leah who, like many of us, tried over and over to please her husband to no avail.

My heart really goes out to Leah, and the Leahs of the world because as I said, at one point I was her. Leah's husband Jacob really wanted to marry her younger sister, Rachel. Jacob had worked for Leah and Rachel's father for seven years to obtain the right to marry Rachel. And the night that Jacob went in to consummate his marriage to Rachel, their father sent Leah into the room instead. When Jacob thought he sealed the deal with Rachel, when he woke up the next morning he found out it was Leah who he ended up marrying. Boy was he disappointed. And rightfully so, as no one wants to be tricked into marrying someone. Well Jacob stayed with Leah and worked another seven years for the right to marry Rachel. So now Jacob is married to both sisters and his disdain for Leah is evident. The bible says that Jacob loved Rachel, but Leah...he tolerated her. Leah tried everything to get Jacob to love her. And when God saw that she was unloved, he caused her to have baby after baby after baby. Hoping that her husband would come around and love her, for the babies' sake. But not even a whole gang of babies could change Jacob's feelings toward his wife.

I remember being Leah. Not feeling loved. Doing everything I knew to get someone just to "see" me, notice me, love me. It's a desperate, lonely place. But God. Even if we're not loved or chosen by man, God loves us and God chooses us. You see, Leah had a baby boy named Judah. And if you read the 1st chapter of the Book of Matthew, you'll see that it's through the lineage of Judah that our Savior, Jesus Christ, was born. Even though Leah was unloved and not Jacob's choice, she was God's choice. It was through Leah and not Rachel that God chose to bring forth His only begotten Son. It was through Leah that God sent His wonderful plan to redeem humanity. It was through Leah that God sent the Light of the world.

So don't be discouraged if you're not picked to be on the team. Don't be upset if he or she leaves you for another. Don't throw in the towel because they didn't like your idea. God has a way of turning things around in our favor. Remember that God loves you with an everlasting love. He wants to fulfill our need to be loved and accepted. He loves us, He accepts us, He chooses us...every day, every time. "For you are a holy people [set apart] to the Lord your God; the Lord your God has chosen you out of all the peoples on the face of the earth to be a people for His own possession [that is, His very special treasure]" (Deuteronomy 7:6, AMP). You may not be man's choice, but you are God's chosen.

Let's Pray:

Heavenly Father, I thank you so much that I am loved and chosen by you. Nothing feels better than knowing that the Creator of the universe loves me. I thank you for your unconditional love. Please help me to remember that I am complete in you and that I don't have to seek the approval or love of others. I am secure in your love for me. And I take comfort in knowing that absolutely nothing can separate me from your love (Romans 8:38-39). In Jesus' name, Amen.

A Call To Action:

What has God said to you about today's devotional?

What things can you do, or what steps can you take to apply today's devotional?

DAY 15:
TEAMWORK MAKES THE DREAM WORK

(Key Passage: Psalm 133:1-3)

"Behold, how good and how pleasant it is for brethren to dwell together in unity!"

Psalm 133:1 (NKJV)

While working at my old job, my former boss thought it was a good idea to get some leadership training for those employees who were considered managers and above. He felt that we would be his leadership team and help with the direction of the firm. He brought in outside consultants to help with the training. During that training, we were given an assignment to read *The Five Dysfunctions of a Team*, by Patrick Lencioni. I thought the book was fascinating and it really helped shape my understanding of the importance of working as a team. So much so that I often refer to it when I'm teaching on team-building at my church. I've even come up with my own version of five pillars for successful teams, using the word of God.

It is so important for believers to know that God made us to be a part of a body. And as a body we're much larger than a team, but we are still connected to one another, and our collective success is directly related to our individual successes. 1 Corinthians chapter 12 talks about the unity and diversity in the body of Christ. It says we are one body that's made up of many parts. Like our physical bodies are made up of eyes, ears, legs, arms, etc. So too the body (the collective church) is made up of different parts (pastors, teachers, ushers, musicians) and each part has its own function or gift. And in order for the church body to function at its optimal level, all the members (parts) must stay healthy so they can do their part. The Bible stresses that each part is needed and that no part can say there is no need of another part. It says that God has put this body (the church) together just as He wants it to be. And we should honor each part so that there is no division in the body.

It's really an amazing thing that God has done. In His omniscience, He made it so that none of us could exclude any of us. This all-for-one and one-for-all concept is to be maintained throughout the body. Regardless of color, age, economic status, what country you live in, or even what continent you live on. If you are a child of God, then you are a part of the body. With our different languages and cultures, backgrounds and experiences, preferences and biases, God calls us His body—one body.

Do you sometimes feel alone with no one to talk to? I encourage you, find your brothers and sisters in Christ and connect with other members of the body. God has placed on the inside of you a gift that the body needs. He's given you an idea that the body is waiting on. We are better together. I've often heard people use the excuse that they've been hurt by "the church." Please don't think I'm trying to minimize your pain at all. I am certain that there have been some people within the body who haven't always acted Christ-like. And I pray earnestly for people like that. I'm also praying for you, that God would heal you to recover from the hurt. Because both are missing out on so much. You are missing out on the beautiful fellowship with other believers, and they're missing out on the talent that God has blessed you with for the body. That's why grace and forgiveness are so important if the body is going to remain unified. God says if we don't forgive others, He won't forgive us (Matthew 6:15). So if you are that person who has been hurt by somebody or somebodies in the church, ask God to help you forgive them and heal your wounds. Then find your way back to a church where you can freely worship and join in the fellowship with your church family.

God commands His blessing when there is unity. The devil wants to keep us separated, divided and at odds with one another. I've read that Sunday mornings are still the most segregated time in our country. I take that as an indictment against God's body. I know we all have our preferences for worship style, music, preaching and the like. But at some point we should be able to come together, putting all differences aside and unite around the one thing we all have in common—Jesus Christ and His lordship in our lives. So reach out to a brother or sister you haven't spoken to in a while. Go to church with someone you wouldn't typically go with. Visit another area or culture to see how they experience worship. I'm sure you'll find something that you can say "Amen" to. Like Hezekiah Walker wrote in the lyrics to his song, "I need you, you need me, we're all a part of God's body. Stand with me, agree with me, we're all a part of God's body. It is His will that every need be supplied. You are important to me, I need you to survive."

Let's Pray:

O God, thank you for the blessedness of unity. Thank you for placing me in a body with others. God, I know that we all have gifts and talents to share with one another. Help me to always remember that you created me to be a part of a larger body. Remind me to reach out and check in on those I haven't seen in a while and to remind them that they are needed. In Jesus' name, Amen.

A Call To Action:

What has God said to you about today's devotional?

What things can you do, or what steps can you take to apply today's devotional?

DAY 16:
IF I CAN HELP SOMEBODY

(Key Passage: Luke 22:31-38)

"Simon, Simon (Peter), listen. Satan has demanded permission to sift [all of] you like grain; but I have prayed [especially] for you [Peter], that your faith [and confidence in Me] may not fail; and you, once you have turned back again [to Me], strengthen and support your brothers [in the faith]."

Luke 22:31-32 (AMP)

In 2001 I decided to go to law school, after ten years of being out of school. No one in my family was a lawyer, and I didn't personally know any lawyers. But based on what I saw on TV, I thought being a lawyer would be cool. I also was a single parent of two and working full-time in tax when I decided to go back. Needless to say, law school was a challenge: working all day, running home to take care of the kids, then back out to law school in the evenings... oh and summer classes too. Whew. I'm tired just thinking about it again. But thanks to the tremendous support of family and friends, I graduated in 2005 and passed both the Pennsylvania and New Jersey bar exams. I had practiced law for about 5 months before I knew it was not for me. So back to tax I went. Someone once asked me why I went through all the trouble of going to law school, especially with everything else I had going on in my life. Why write all those papers, take all those exams, study and sit for two state bar exams only to give it up? Don't you feel like it was a waste of time, energy and effort, not to mention money? My response? Absolutely not.

You see it was not that expensive for me because my job paid for a large portion of my tuition. But also I enjoyed every bit of law school. Met interesting people and learned about interesting topics. I learned how to write persuasively crafted legal documents. I learned the workings of the criminal justice system and a little about immigration. I learned about tort law, contracts, medical malpractice and the rules of evidence. Law school was cool. The practice of law, not so much.

My time in law school tested my strength, endurance, time management skills and intellect. It showed me that I could achieve whatever I put my mind to if I wanted it bad enough. And those lessons can never be taken from me. But the bigger reason why I don't regret law school is the number of young people, male and female, that I have been able to motivate and encourage. They've looked to me as a source of inspiration while they were either considering or going through law school. They've considered me an adviser and have drawn from my experiences and knowledge. Not much beats the feeling of knowing you've helped someone through a difficult and sometimes scary time. Every phone call, lunch and letter of recommendation fed my passion for helping others, giving me a sense of pride that I've helped a future generation of legal minds. I believe that's what life is all about. After we've been helped, to reach back and help someone else.

Jesus told Peter that Satan wanted to destroy all of Jesus' disciples. But He said He prayed especially for Peter (Peter would be the rock of the church, Matthew 16:18.) that his faith would not fail. He told Peter that after he was strengthened, then don't forget to strengthen and support your brothers (and sisters) in the faith (Luke 22:32). I'm sure Peter was able to encourage other believers who were going through times of adversity because he too had been through tough times and prevailed. What a blessing to know that you can encourage someone else because of something you've been through.

I don't know what challenges in life you've had to come through. But I'm confident that whatever it was, somebody else is going through (or will go through) the same thing. And your testimony can serve as a source of great comfort and encouragement to lift up someone else. Sometimes we go through things not for ourselves, but for other people. So share your successes and challenges, your ups and downs, your highs and your lows. You never know who you will inspire by what you've been through.

Let's Pray:

Dear Jesus, thank you for every experience in my life. The good, the bad and the ugly...I know that you have a purpose for it all. Help me to be willing to share my experiences with others as you lead me to, so that I can help someone else through a difficult time. Thank you that I have your Holy Spirit to help me in times of trouble. I desire to be a blessing to others, continue to use me. In Jesus' name, Amen.

A Call To Action:

What has God said to you about today's devotional?

What things can you do, or what steps can you take to apply today's devotional?

DAY 17:
THE DEAD DOG SYNDROME

(Key Passage: 2 Samuel 9:1-13)

"Then he bowed himself, and said,
'What is your servant, that you should look upon
such a dead dog as I?'"

2 Samuel 9:8 (NKJV)

For a long time I suffered from low self-esteem. I didn't see myself as talented or having any special gifts. I'll never forget a supervisor I had at one of my first jobs. I worked in an area with a lot of other young people. I desperately wanted them to like me so I went to lunch with them, took breaks with them, even spent time with a few of them outside of work. I remember when I first got the job and how excited I was. I bought new work clothes, suits, slacks, shoes and blouses. But I quickly realized none of my new friends "dressed up" for work; they wore jeans, sneakers and even sweatpants. So I ditched my newly bought clothes and started wearing my jeans and sneakers. After a while my supervisor came to me, telling me she noticed the change, not only in my clothing but also in my behavior. Then she said something I'll never forget. She said,

"LaVon, you're not like those other girls. There's something different about you. I can see you're smart and very talented. Don't let them bring you down." I was shocked. *How dare she talk down about my new friends. There was nothing special about me. I'm one of them*, were my thoughts. My low self-esteem wouldn't allow me to believe anything good or special about myself. I'd come to find out years and years later that my old supervisor was right. I was different, special and talented. I may have left that job long ago, but her words are still with me today.

Mephibosheth needed a supervisor like that in his life, and King David came to his rescue. You'll have to read all the way back to 1 Samuel chapter 18 to get the full story. But Jonathan was the son of King Saul and David's best friend. Saul and Jonathan were dead at that point, but David wanted to honor them by blessing someone from their lineage. He asked his servants to find someone from the "house of Saul" that he could show kindness to. David's servant told him that Jonathan had a son named Mephibosheth who was alive and living in a place called Lo-debar. King David went to Lo-debar, found Mephibosheth and told him that he's restoring to him all the land that belonged to his father and grandfather and that from that point forward, Mephibosheth would be allowed to eat with David, the king. Mephibosheth's response to David lets me know he too suffered from low self-esteem. Mephibosheth, bowed down and said to David, "What am I that you would show this kind of favor to me? I'm nothing but a dead dog." Yup, that's low self-esteem talking.

So what would cause Mephibosheth, the grandson of a king, to have low self-esteem? It was where he lived and what he had. Or better said, it was the way Mephibosheth saw and felt about where he lived and what he had. Lo-debar was considered the "ghetto" in the town of Gilead. And the Bible tells us that Mephibosheth was lame in both of his feet. So this descendant of a king looked at his surroundings and his condition and determined that he wasn't worthy to eat with the king. *I'm from the ghetto and I have a disability. I'm nothing more than a dead dog* is what Mephibosheth thought. He didn't believe he deserved anything that King David wanted to bless him with.

How many times have you played yourself small because of something about you that makes you feel unworthy? Even when someone else is trying to get you to see just how beautiful, amazing, strong, talented or wise you are. You can't see past where you live, your disability, your criminal record, your children out of wedlock or your lack of finances, your failed marriage, your mother's death or your lack of education. The excuses we give to ourselves keep us from "eating at the King's table." David told Mephibosheth that he would be treated just like one of his very own sons. And God is saying to you and me, we are His children just like His own Son. See yourself as God sees you. You are not where you live. You are not that disease or disability you have. You are not what society calls you. You are not what your criminal record says. You are not those names your father called you. You are not a victim. You are not unqualified. You are not timid. YOU ARE A CHILD OF GOD! Don't accept the "dead dog" labels that your conditions or others have placed on you. Reject every name, label or identity that goes against what God says about you. God calls you healed. God calls you blessed. God calls you worthy. God calls you righteous. God calls you talented. God calls you forgiven. God calls you His masterpiece. God calls you loved. Today take your rightful place at the King's table where you'll dine with Him continually.

Let's Pray:

Father God, I thank you for calling me righteous. I thank you that today I am free from all the negative stereotypes I have accepted and called myself by. I no longer am identified by those names and I accept my new name, Redeemed. Thank you, Jesus for making me righteous in God's sight. In Jesus' name, Amen.

A Call To Action:

What has God said to you about today's devotional?

What things can you do, or what steps can you take to apply today's devotional?

DAY 18:
GOD'S LOVE LANGUAGE

(Key Passage: Micah 6:1-8)

"He has shown you, O man what is good; and what does the LORD require of you but to do justly, to love mercy, and to walk humbly with your God?"

Micah 6:8 (NKJV)

During premarital counseling, my husband-to-be and I were given an assignment to read the book, *The Five Love Languages*, by Gary Chapman. Boy was that book eye-opening. It taught us to pay attention to and understand how each other gives, and likes to receive, love. According to Chapman, there are five primary love languages: Receiving Gifts, Physical Touch, Acts of Service, Words of Affirmation and Quality Time. My husband's primary love language is words of affirmation, in that he likes to hear words that compliment and praise him, reaffirming that I love him and value him in our relationship. My primary love language is acts of service. I like my husband to show his love for me by doing things for me: housework, getting my car cleaned, going grocery shopping, etc.

In the early years of our relationship we struggled with trying to please each other because we weren't speaking each other's love language. So while my husband would buy flowers, or hold hands, or tell me how beautiful I was, it didn't really give me the warm and fuzzy feeling like he had hoped because that wasn't my love language. And while I worked at doing the laundry and doing the shopping to show my love for my husband, he still felt unappreciated because I didn't verbalize it with words of affirmation. But after reading that book and working at trying to understand and implement its concepts, a mutual love and appreciation for each other developed. Now I know that I can't go too long without telling my man that he's doing a wonderful job and that he's appreciated. And he works hard at helping around the house and getting my car washed. I'm still working on getting him to do the grocery shopping though, LOL.

In the 6th chapter of the Book of Micah, the Lord is making a complaint against His people, Israel. God's people had gone astray time and time again by serving other gods and turning their backs on the true God. They were taking advantage of the poor; they were proud and boastful; they treated their workers harshly. Yet they continued to offer sacrifice and burnt offerings to God to fulfill their traditions and rituals as a way to appease God. All the while their hearts were far from God. So God told them through the prophet Micah, I don't want your meaningless sacrifices and burnt offerings; I want your hearts.

Micah warned Israel that God had shown them what He desires; He told them what would please Him. And it was not in the amount of money they gave or even if they were to give their first born child.

I've heard it said that obedience is God's love language. Well there were three things that God wanted Israel to be obedient in doing—do justly, love mercy and walk humbly with God. Israel wanted to give God what was easy for them and what they thought He would want. But God said, "No, what I desire is for you to treat people with justice." God desired that they show mercy to the poor and oppressed. God wanted them to be meek and humble. He wanted them to treat others the way He had treated them—loving them, taking care of them, being patient with them.

In Matthew 23:23 (Christian Standard Bible), Jesus warned the Pharisees of a similar offense. When they were proud and puffed up about how much they were giving in the temple, Jesus said to them, "Woe to you, scribes and Pharisees, hypocrites. You pay a tenth of mint, dill, and cumin, and yet you have neglected the more important matters of the law—justice, mercy, and faithfulness. These things should have been done without neglecting the others." Let us not neglect what God requires—justice, mercy, humility. What injustices can you speak out against? Who can you show mercy to? Where do you need to humble yourself? That's how we show God we understand His love language.

Let's Pray:

Dear Lord, I apologize for the times when I've given you what I wanted to give you, instead of what you required me to give. Holy Spirit, make me sensitive to God's love language and to those things that He desires of me. And then help me to have a willing heart and mind to do them. Father, I want to please you because you have done so much for me and have given me so much. Doing the things you require is how I will show my love and appreciation for you. In Jesus' name, Amen.

A Call To Action:

What has God said to you about today's devotional?

____

____

____

____

____

____

____

____

What things can you do, or what steps can you take to apply today's devotional?

____

____

____

____

____

____

____

____

____

DAY 19:
SPIRITUAL ADDITION

(Key Passage: 2 Peter 1:1-11)

*"So devote yourselves to lavishly supplementing your faith with goodness, and to goodness **add** understanding, and to understanding **add** the strength of self-control, and to self-control **add** patient endurance, and to patient endurance, **add** godliness, and to godliness **add** mercy toward your brothers and sisters, and to mercy toward others **add** unending love." (emphasis mine)*

2 Peter 1:5-7 (The Passion Translation)

I like problem solving. My brain works best with order and structure. I used to think that it was because the left side of my brain (where our logic resides) was the most dominant. But recently I read an article that suggests all that left-brained/right-brained stuff is a myth. However it seems to at least be partially true because the left-brained/right-brained theory says that left-brained individuals' strengths are things like math, analytics, reading, problem-solving and spelling—all the things I'm good at. They also say right-brained individuals' strengths include visualization and abstract thinking—all things I'm not good at. At any rate, whether it's true or not, math, science and spelling were among my favorite classes in school. I was naturally good at them. My favorite math class was Algebra II. The equations and the formulas—I loved it. I think I liked the finality of math. There usually was a definite right or wrong answer. It wasn't subjective. It didn't matter how I *felt* about the problem; it only mattered that I came to the right conclusion.

In today's passage of scripture, Peter gives us some spiritual math, whereby we can reach a definite conclusion if we follow the equation. As believers we are called to grow in the grace and knowledge of God. After we become saved, we should not remain in the same place, at the "new convert" level. We should be growing higher and deeper in God. I know people who have been saved for many years, yet their lives and conduct don't add up to how a mature Christian should live and/or behave. Please don't take this as being judgmental. It's just that almost everything grows—babies, trees, our hair. And if something that's supposed to grow isn't, we say there's something wrong with it. So all of us should be looking to grow and mature in our walk with Christ. Even Peter says in 1 Peter 2:2 (NIV), "Like newborn babies, crave pure spiritual milk, so that by it you may grow up in your salvation." When we don't grow, we miss out on enjoying everything that God has for us.

So Peter provides us with a list of things we can add to our new faith so that we can grow in our knowledge of God. When we get saved, God gives each of us a degree of faith. But it will take more than that initial degree to keep us through the tough times of life. So Peter says to do some spiritual addition and add more to our degree of faith. First he says add goodness. The King James version of the Bible uses the word "virtue," and other translations use the word "moral excellence." What it basically means is conformity to a standard of right, having a sense of doing right and living right in the world with the standard being set by the word of God. After goodness Peter says we should add understanding or knowledge. This means general knowledge of the Christian faith. We should seek to understand our faith—what we believe, why we believe it, the foundational truths.

After understanding we should add self-control. Self-control is part of the fruit of the Spirit. When we can practice self-control, it is evidence that Holy Spirit is working and active in you. It takes a mature person to practice self-control and deny him or herself of worldly pleasures to seek the things of God. We should add to self-control patience. Patience implies having endurance. A lot of us have the "microwave mentality" in that we don't want to wait for anything. I want what I want, and I want it now. But Peter says in this walk we need to learn how to endure, be patient, wait it out.

Add to our patience, godliness. Godliness is a reverence and respect for God and His word. When we reverence God, we'll become sensitive to the things that displease Him. Proverbs

9:10 says, "The fear of the Lord is the beginning of wisdom." When we reverence God we start to become wise. We then should add to godliness mercy for our brothers and sisters, or brotherly kindness. We should cherish our Christian brothers and sisters and treat them kindly and hospitably, recognizing that they are part of our new family. And after we learn how to be merciful and treat our brothers and sisters kindly, we should strive to add love to our walk. You can read 1 Corinthians chapter 13 to learn all about what true agape love is.

Peter says if we add all these things up and keep increasing in them, we will neither be unproductive nor ineffective in our knowledge of Jesus Christ. We'll never stumble and we'll receive a rich welcome into the eternal kingdom of God. Now how's that for an equation? So don't stop growing in your faith. Don't settle for staying where you are. Keep on adding to your faith, you can never add too much. Be diligent about your growth in Christ and the new life you have in Him.

Let's Pray:

Heavenly Father, I want to grow in you. Help me to practice adding to my faith the things that Peter talks about. I want to grow in goodness, knowledge, self-control, patience, godliness, brotherly kindness and love so that one day, you'll welcome me into your eternal kingdom. Help me to live as a mature child of God. In Jesus' name, Amen.

A Call To Action:

What has God said to you about today's devotional?

What things can you do, or what steps can you take to apply today's devotional?

DAY 20:
I AM GRACED TO GIVE

(Key Passage: 2 Corinthians 9:1-15)

*"And God is able to make **all** grace [**every** favor and earthly blessing, come in **abundance** to you, so that you may **always** [under **all** circumstances, regardless of the need] have **complete** sufficiency in **everything** [being **completely** self-sufficient in Him], and have an **abundance** for **every** good work and act of charity." (emphasis mine)*

2 Corinthians 9:8 (AMP)

There are several causes that I'm especially passionate about. Education, children and the word of God, to name a few. And while I have never been employed in any of those fields, I do a lot of volunteering around these areas. It brings me so much joy and pleasure when I know I've helped someone in some small way. Another way that I serve in these areas is by giving to them. But my giving extends beyond just these causes. I've given to St. Jude's Children's Hospital, United Way, Habitat for Humanity and other ministries that serve around the world. I don't mention this to brag in any way. I only bring it up to say that I get great joy in knowing that while I can't do everything for everyone, I can do something for someone. Giving of my time, talent or treasure are some of the ways I show my gratitude to God for blessing me with so much. Now I may not have much by the world's standard of much, but God has always met my every need when I needed Him to.

For me, giving is one of those things that just comes naturally. I've mentioned elsewhere in this devotional that I just love helping people, so giving is one of the ways I help. I support other small businesses—even if I don't personally use their products. I support children by raising money for their schools. I support other ministries that are digging water wells in Africa. And while these things may not directly benefit me, they provide a greater benefit in knowing that I've made a contribution that extends around the world—even if I can't physically be there. Because of this there have been too many instances to count where I've given to someone or some cause and no sooner than I've given, it comes right back to me. Just when I think I've given my last, someone will come along the same day and bless me with an offering. Or when I think our funds are down to the last few dollars, that next day I'll get a new client who gives an up-front retainer. God really does supply all of my need according to His riches in glory (Philippians 4:13).

I want to encourage you to begin seeking ways in which you can support either the causes you're passionate about or just people in general. In today's verse, Paul is thanking the

Corinthians for their kind gifts to him and to the work of the Lord. He lets them know that when you support other people generously, God gives you a special grace so you'll always have whatever you need. I think some people are afraid to give because they think there will be less for them and their needs. But let me encourage you that the Bible says God loves a cheerful giver. And when we give cheerfully, it's an indication of a grateful heart. When we're grateful to God, He blesses us with even more. Now I'm not suggesting that we give just so we can get more. But there is a spiritual principle involved—we reap what we sow. Luke 6:38 (NLT) puts it this way, "Give, and you will receive. Your gift will return to you in full—pressed down, shaken together to make room for more, running over, and poured into your lap. The amount you give will determine the amount you get back."

So don't be afraid to give. Don't be stingy. Be generous. Be charitable. When you purpose in your heart to give, God says you'll always (under all circumstances) have everything you need. You'll have not just enough to get by, but you'll have complete sufficiency (lacking nothing) to abound unto every good work. Go back up and look at today's verse again. Note all the expressions of abundance used. And then go look for someone to bless today. Don't worry, you're graced to give.

Let's Pray:

Dear God, thank you for the opportunity to give. Thank you for giving me more than I need so that I have enough to share with others. I know when I give with a cheerful heart, you'll supply me with everything I need so that I can continue being a blessing to others. Please show me who I can bless today. In Jesus' name, Amen.

A Call To Action:

What has God said to you about today's devotional?

____
____
____
____
____
____
____
____

What things can you do, or what steps can you take to apply today's devotional?

____
____
____
____
____
____
____
____
____

DAY 21:
SING A PSALM

(Key Passage: Psalm 96:1-13)

"O sing unto the LORD a new song:
sing unto the LORD, all the earth."

Psalm 96:1 (KJV)

I love music. Any kind of music (to quote the O'Jays). Gospel, jazz, R&B, musicals, and even a little country. I like old school music, modern, classical and contemporary. Rap music, disco, pop and one or two rock songs. I love music. There are so many wonderfully talented artists who have produced some great music for us to enjoy. Here are some of my personal favorites: Stevie Wonder, Michael Jackson, Whitney Houston, Maurette Brown-Clark, Fred Hammond, Toby Mac, Jonathan McReynolds, Smokie Norful, Chris Tomlin, Luther Vandross, Kellie Clarkson, Jeffrey Osborne, Elevation Worship, Geoffrey Golden, Cody Carnes, Mary Mary, Natalie Grant, Tasha Cobbs-Leonard, Beyoncé, Mary J. Blige, John Legend and Myron Butler. And more recently I've been enjoying Todd Dulaney, Chandler Moore & Maverick City, and Lauren Daigle. Did I mention I love music?

I love singing and dancing to music. But very often, I don't need music. I'll sing and dance to a song in my head and heart. That's why I have no problem with Psalm 96:1. I can make up a song—my own words and my own beat—and sing all throughout the house. I wake up most mornings with a song on my heart and I thank God for that. And even though I'm not a great singer when I'm worshiping God it doesn't matter. I don't have to hit the right key or sing in tune. I can be loud or quiet. I can hum or whistle.

Scientists and researchers have studied the effect music has on people and the benefits are amazing. From increased concentration to higher SAT scores, from greater problem solving skills to being a more efficient worker, from helping our bodies recover faster to distracting the body from pain—yes, the effects of music are astounding.

God loves music too. The Bible admonishes us in several places to sing unto the Lord and to sing to one another. He knows the power of music and He encourages us to sing and dance and play instruments. And if for some reason you can't find any music that gets you excited, then create your own. The Book of Psalms is a collection of songs. Songs of triumph, victory, encouragement, deliverance and much more. And who can't get excited about that. I'll get you started with a few of my favorites.

- But Thou, O Lord, are a shield for me, my glory and the lifter up of my head. (Psalm 3:3)

- Thou will show me the path of life; in Thy presence is the fullness of joy; at Thy right hand there are pleasures forevermore. (Psalm 16:11)
- The Lord is my light and my salvation; whom shall I fear? The Lord is the strength of my life; of whom shall I be afraid? (Psalm 27:1)
- I will bless the Lord at all times: His praise shall continually be in my mouth. (Psalm 34:1)
- From the end of the earth will I cry unto thee, when my heart is overwhelmed: lead me to the rock that is higher than I. (Psalm 61:2)
- Thy way, O God, is in the sanctuary: who is so great a God as our God? Thou art the God that doest wonders: Thou has declared Thy strength among the people (Psalm 77:13-14)
- It is a good thing to give thanks unto the Lord, and to sing praises unto thy name, O Most High (Psalm 92:1)
- Praise ye the Lord. I will praise the Lord with my whole heart, in the assembly of the upright, and in the congregation. (Psalm 111:1)
- Let everything that has breath praise the Lord. Praise ye the Lord. (Psalm 150:6)

So start singing. Add your own verses. Pull a verse or two out of your favorite Psalms. Or better yet, make up your own psalm to the Lord. I'm sure God has been so good to you that you've got a verse of your own that hasn't been written yet. At a minimum, if you're saved by the blood of Jesus, you can sing the song of the redeemed. Revelation 5:9 (NASB) states, "And they sang a new song, saying, 'Worthy are You to take the book and to break its seals; for You were slain, and purchased for God with Your blood men from every tribe and tongue and people and nation.'"

Let's Pray:

Heavenly Father, thank you for the gift of music. Thank you for putting a new song in my heart each day. As I go about my day and remember your goodness, I'll sing your praises throughout the day. I love you, Lord, and I love to sing praises to your name. In Jesus' name, Amen.

A Call To Action:

What has God said to you about today's devotional?

What things can you do, or what steps can you take to apply today's devotional?

DAY 22:
WHICH WAY SHOULD I GO?

(Key Passage: Psalm 37:1-25)

"The steps of a [good and righteous] man are directed and established by the LORD, and He delights in his way [and blesses his path]."

Psalm 37:23 (AMP)

Ever since I can remember I've wanted to be a teacher. I have vivid memories of "playing school" with my sister and brother where I was the teacher and they were the students. I'd give them homework assignments and mark their test papers. I thoroughly enjoyed everything about school back then. But somewhere along the line, I decided to pursue accounting when I went to college. When it was time for me to pick a major, I didn't do any soul searching. I didn't go back and remember the joy I used to get while "teaching" my sister and brother. Instead I chose what came easily for me, and what would provide the most money upon graduation. I had taken a bookkeeping class in high school and excelled at it. So I selected accounting as a major, as that was the closest to bookkeeping; and I'd heard that you could make a lot of money in it. But every now and again, I wonder what my life would have been like had I pursued a career in education. Now that's not to say that my chosen field has not afforded me some wonderful opportunities. I've met some amazing people, visited some pretty cool places and worked on some interesting assignments. I've even had the opportunity to teach a few courses; but most importantly, I've made life-long friendships with people who I wouldn't have met otherwise. And for that I'm eternally grateful. But I still wonder.

Today I am a Sunday School and Bible Study teacher at my church and I love it. Very little gives me more satisfaction. So today's verse is near and dear to my heart. Because God knew all along how much I loved teaching. When I began to listen to what He wanted me to do instead of doing things on my own, He made a way for me to do what I love. I know He has directed my steps and has blessed my path.

What about you? Are you doing what you love? Are you living your dream? If not, why not? The Bible says that God directs and establishes our steps. When we surrender our plans to Him, He causes them to be established (Proverbs 16:3). As you're deciding what to do in life, keep God in the equation. Don't do what I did, don't allow ease and money to be the determining factors for doing something. Be guided by what God has put in your heart. What are you passionate about? What brings you the most joy? What are you good at? What are your natural talents and abilities? Seek out those things and commit them to the Lord. Is it animals or carpentry? What about science or architecture? Traveling the world and blogging about it? Perhaps it's music or opening a boarding house for runaway teens? Whatever it is, don't be afraid to go after it.

Some of you may be thinking it's too late for you, or that you're too old to switch careers or try something new. I'm here to tell you that you're never too old, and it's never too late. As long as God continues to wake you up each day with health and strength, you can live out your dreams. Don't allow fear, doubt or worry to keep you from pursuing what you love. I still work as an accountant, but I have my own practice with much more flexible hours. And I have so much more time and freedom to do what I love, which is teach. You should see me researching topics for Bible Study and coming up with ways to make the lessons engaging and fun. My first book, *Fire New*, actually started out as a Bible Study series I was going to teach until the Holy Spirit said to turn it into a book. So you never know what will become of your life when you commit your works to the Lord. Never in a million years would I have thought I'd be an author and now I've written two books.

So I just want to encourage you that your steps are ordered by God. Listen to His still, small voice for direction. You don't need to stumble through life wondering what to do or become. Pay attention to the tugging on your heart. Remember the fairy tale Hansel and Gretel? It's really a very sad story. But what I remember is that they would leave bread crumbs on the trail to find their way back home. You and I don't need bread crumbs to guide us. God is our compass. He directs us through the twists and turns of life, all the while establishing our steps and blessing our paths.

Let's Pray:

Dear God, I thank you for leading me and guiding me through life. I'm sorry for the times when I didn't acknowledge you in my ways. Help me to get back on track with you. Show me what you would have me to do. I commit my life and my works into your hands. Bring order to my life. Bless my steps as I bring them in alignment with you and your word. In Jesus' name, Amen.

A Call To Action:

What has God said to you about today's devotional?

What things can you do, or what steps can you take to apply today's devotional?

DAY 23:
DON'T GET COMFORTABLE WITH THE CANAANITES

(Key Passage: Judges 1:19-34)

"When the Israelites grew stronger, they forced the Canaanites to work as slaves, but they never did drive them completely out of the land."

Judges 1:28 (NLT)

I am one of those people who floss constantly. I instantly notice when the tiniest particle is stuck between my teeth. This may be no big deal for others, but I cannot be comfortable unless it's dislodged. It drives me crazy when I can't get to a piece of dental floss or a toothpick. I'll try anything to get rid of it—suck my teeth, use a piece of string from my clothing, pick at it with my fingernail—I mean anything. I can't concentrate on anything else until the food particle is gone, and once it's gone, the feeling is so freeing.

While having food stuck between your teeth may not be uncomfortable for you, having fear stuck between you and God's promise for your life should be. Let me explain. When God freed the children of Israel from Pharaoh and the Egyptians,

He made them a promise that he would bring them into a promised land, a land flowing with milk and honey (Exodus 3:8). And all throughout the forty years they spent in the wilderness, God kept reminding them of that promise. When Moses died and Joshua became their leader, again and again God reminded them of the land that He promised them. However the land was already occupied by other nations: Canaanites, Hittites, Perizzites, Lions, Tigers, Bears, oh my. In order for the Israelites to inherit the land, they would have to fight and drive out those other nations. But no problem, God's promises are sure, so let's go. Joshua started leading this military effort of destroying those other nations and possessing the territory that God promised. But then Joshua died, and there was no one person to lead this effort. The children of Israel seemed to begin to forget God and His promises. They drove out some of the inhabitants but not all of them.

Why did Israel fall short of driving out all of the inhabitants as God told them to do? I believe a big reason was that they became comfortable with those other nations living among them. When we become too comfortable with our surroundings, it hinders us from pushing forward. And in Israel's case, their comfortability and complacency was a detriment to them. You see those other nations served strange gods, worshiped idols and drew Israel away from serving the one true God. They caused Israel to stray in their walk with God and they got comfortable with having obtained only a part of the promise. God said to drive all those nations out of the land, but Israel allowed the Canaanites to live among them.

If God has made us a promise, we should not be satisfied with only a portion of it. Don't allow a little good success to keep you from striving for God's ultimate success. Don't be comfortable with letting people hang around when God says cut them off. Don't give in and accept your sickness when God says you're healed. Don't allow other people's opinions about you to limit what you do when God says He's given everything you need for life and godliness. If we are going to reach our promised land, we have to drive out the "Canaanites"—comfortability, fear, doubt, worry, negative thoughts and sometimes people. But with God on our side, we can conquer anything. Romans 8:18 (Contemporary English Version) says, "I am sure what we are suffering now cannot compare with the glory that will be shown to us." Go get your promise, drive out the Canaanites and possess your land that flows with milk and honey.

Let's Pray:

Dear God, thank you for my promised land. Help me to see the "Canaanites" that I've not completely driven away. Holy Spirit, help me to have the courage to get rid of anything that stands in the way of me obtaining the full promise of God's word. I don't want to be comfortable with having a little when God wants to give me much. Father, thank you for reminding me that all of your promises are Yes and Amen in you (2 Corinthians 1:20). In Jesus' Name, Amen.

A Call To Action:

What has God said to you about today's devotional?

What things can you do, or what steps can you take to apply today's devotional?

DAY 24:
WHAT ARE YOU DOING HERE?

(Key Passage: 1 Kings 18–19:1–18)

"And there he went into a cave, and spent the night in that place; and behold, the word of the Lord came to him, and He said to him, 'What are you doing here, Elijah?'"

1 Kings 19:9 (NKJV)

I am directionally-challenged. I have no sense of direction—north, south, east or west, it's all the same to me. If you dropped me in the middle of a forest, I would be forever lost. That's why I am so grateful for the global positioning system (GPS). It allows me to travel more freely and with less anxiety. But boy oh boy, if my cell phone battery ever dies, or if I'm in an area where there is no signal, well, let's just say, go ahead and start dinner without me, LOL. If I'm not careful, the GPS will take me someplace I hadn't intended to go. I blindly turn left and turn right as it directs me to without paying attention to the street or neighborhood I'm in. Never realizing that I want to go to East Norris Street, but it took me to West Norris Street. All I can do is say to myself, "How did I end up here?" Have you ever been there? If you have, then you'll enjoy today's passage of scripture. But if you're good with directions and have never been lost, you'll enjoy it as well.

Elijah, the prophet of God, found himself running for his life, hiding in a cave...from a woman. This was a man who spoke with God, a man that prayed for the rain to stop and it did, a man God used to perform all kinds of miracles. But yet Elijah found himself hiding and God had to ask him, "What are you doing here, Elijah?" Why was Elijah so afraid of a woman? Because he *saw* what she *said.* You read it right, he saw what she said, and not, he *heard* what she *said.* Let me explain.

God's people Israel, were in a depraved state. They had an up and down relationship with God and at this time, they were down. Erecting idols, worshiping other gods, doing whatever they wanted and paying God no mind. God raised up Elijah as a prophet to warn Israel to turn from their wicked ways and turn back to God. So Elijah was doing his thing, prophesying against Israel's kings and in doing so, God used Elijah to work miracles to show God's power. On one occasion Elijah challenged the current king, Ahab, to a fire burning contest in an effort to prove that Elijah's God was the true God. It was Elijah and his prophets against Ahab and his prophets. The challenge was to get a bull, cut it in pieces and lay it on wood. Whichever God answered by fire and burned up the bull on the wood would be considered the true God. Ahab went first and called on his god Baal—nothing happened. Ahab and his prophets yelled and shouted for their god to bring the fire, still nothing. When it was Elijah's turn, to highlight God's power even further, he drowned the bull in water first. Then Elijah called on his God and of course, God answered and burned up the bull. So the people rejoiced and proclaimed that Elijah's God is the true God. Elijah then had all of Ahab's prophets killed.

Well Ahab went home to cry to his wife, Jezebel about what happened. Jezebel sent word to Elijah that she was going to kill him. The Bible says that when Elijah "*saw*" that, he got up and ran for his life. The prophet of God who had just performed a miracle for God heard the words of Jezebel, and his mind formed a picture of her words, and all he could see was her killing him. Even though it hadn't happened, even though he knew he was the prophet of God, even though God had come through for him many times before. Elijah allowed Jezebel's words to cause him to doubt God, fear for his life and go hide in a cave. Until God said, "What are you doing here, Elijah?"

Has anyone ever said something to you that you took to heart that caused you to see what they said? Perhaps they said, "You'll never be anything." and you believed that and are not doing anything with your life. Maybe they said, "You're not smart enough to do that job." And now you won't even submit the job application. Well, I'm here to tell you to stop running and hiding from those lies. God has mapped out your future and it's a future full of hope and promise (Jeremiah 29:11). Don't allow anyone's words to define you. I don't care who they are, or how powerful they may think they are. No one is greater than our God, and He alone determines our destiny. If God called you to do something, He will make sure it happens. Don't listen to the "Jezebels" in your life. God *for you* is greater than the whole world *against you*. "Greater is He that is in you, than he that is in the world" (1 John 4:4). No more running, no more hiding—get out of this cave and go be who God created you to be.

Let's Pray:

Heavenly Father, I need your help right now. There are so many voices in my head and they're causing me to doubt and to fear. Help me to see who I am in you. Help me to see who you're making me to be. Holy Spirit, remind me to be strong in the Lord and in the power of His might according to Ephesians 6:10. In Jesus' name, Amen.

A Call To Action:

What has God said to you about today's devotional?

What things can you do, or what steps can you take to apply today's devotional?

DAY 25:
I GOT THE POWER

(Key Passage: John 10:1-18)

"Therefore My Father loves Me, because I lay down My life that I may take it again. No one takes it from Me, but I lay it down of Myself. I have power to lay it down, and I have power to take it again. This command I have received from My Father."

John 10:17-18 (NKJV)

In 2009 Forbes produced an article titled, "By The Numbers: The World's Most Powerful Things." In the article they list several things that were considered the most powerful, at least at that time. For example the list had the U.S.S.R.'s Big Ivan Bomb as the most powerful weapon, the Great Chilean Earthquake of 1960 was the most powerful earthquake recorded, and at the time, the Roadrunner by IBM was the most powerful computer. I was intrigued by the most powerful poison, Botulinum toxin. The article said the medical uses of this powerful poison were to fight wrinkles and scars, as with Botox, Dysport and Myobloc. Then it said, "Also used as a biological warfare agent." Now I don't know about you, but my wrinkles aren't so bad that I need a biological warfare agent to get rid of them, LOL. But I digress... The article said that one gram of Botulinum toxin could kill 1 million people. It's sometimes scary to think of someone having in their possession something that could wipe out a large population of humanity. But I know someone who has within His being the power to wipe out *all* of humanity; yet, He chose instead to lay down His life for humanity.

Jesus Christ, the only begotten Son of God, is that someone. And the scripture for today reminds us just how powerful He is. In the 10th chapter of the Book of John, Jesus describes Himself as The Good Shepherd. He talks about how He cares for His sheep (you and I); He knows His sheep, and they know Him. He says when the wolf comes (anything or anyone who tries to devour the sheep), a hired helper will desert the sheep because he's only in it for money. But The Good Shepherd will protect the sheep with His life. Jesus then goes on to mention this power that He has. He says that He is loved by His Father because He lays down His life so that He can take it up again. And that He has *power* to lay down His life, and *power* to take it back up.

Oftentimes we focus on the resurrection power of Jesus—the power to take His life up again. But Jesus says it also takes power to lay it down. That really struck a chord with me. In order for something to get back up, it must first go down—and it takes power to do both. For you and me to experience Jesus' resurrection power in our lives, we must activate that same power to lay down our lives. Not literally of course, but we must be willing to lay down those things that are not like God. We must lay down those things that keep us from having true intimacy with him. We must be willing to give up those relationships that cause us to compromise our Christian values. We must give up those attitudes and behaviors that aren't becoming a child of God. We have the power. Power to lay down addiction; power to lay down anger and jealousy; power to lay down pride and greed. We have the power through Jesus Christ. The Passion Translation of Hebrews 12:1 puts it this way, "As for us, we have all of these great witnesses who encircle us like clouds. So we must let go of every wound that has pierced us and the sin we so easily fall into. Then we will be able to run life's marathon race with passion and determination, for the path has already been marked out before us."

My friend, let's use the power that Jesus had, the power He has given us to live for Him. The same power it takes to trample over serpents and scorpions is the same power it takes to love our enemies. The same power it takes to speak to the mountain is the same power it takes to bless and not curse our brother or sister. The same power it takes to triumph over the enemy is the same power it takes to resist him. Most powerful people don't always display humility and compassion. But you and I, by God's grace, are given power to be like Jesus. Let's use our power for good and not evil. My friend, you've got the power.

Let's Pray:

Heavenly Father, thank you for the example of Jesus. I thank you that He has given me overcoming, victorious, mountain moving power. But I also thank you that He has given me power to be loving, kind, merciful and gentle. Help me to stir up that power in times of anxiety, disappointment or even anger. Let me never forget that you are the source of true power. In Jesus' name, Amen.

A Call To Action:

What has God said to you about today's devotional?

What things can you do, or what steps can you take to apply today's devotional?

DAY 26:
STAY WOKE

(Key Passage: Matthew 25:1-13)

"At that time the kingdom of heaven will be like ten virgins who took their lamps and went out to meet the bridegroom. Five of them were foolish and five of them were wise. The foolish ones took their lamps but did not take any oil with them. The wise ones, however, took oil in jars along with their lamps."

Matthew 25:1-4 (NIV)

A documentary entitled "Stay Woke: Black Lives Matter Movement" was released sometime in 2016. The documentary gives a deeper understanding of how the Black Lives Matter movement came about and shares what the movement believes. During that time the expression "stay woke" was used when referring to a perceived awareness concerning social and racial injustice issues. When someone is "woke" they are perceived to be consciously awake to social, racial or even economic injustices that plague our society and particularly those in the black community.

In the 24th chapter of the Book of Matthew, we find Jesus having a "stay woke" moment with His disciples. The entire chapter deals with a conversation Jesus has with His disciples about signs of the end times. He tells them to be aware when they start to hear of "wars and rumors of wars." He tells them to perk up when they start to see and hear of famines and earthquakes in various places. And pay close attention when nation starts to rise against nation, and kingdom against kingdom. For all of these are signs that the end times are soon to come. Jesus told the disciples that no one except God Himself knows exactly when He will return. So He stressed that it was best for them to stay prepared, that way, they wouldn't be caught off guard by His coming and miss out. Then in the 25th chapter, Jesus shares a parable to highlight the danger of being caught unaware, or more importantly, unprepared during that time. The Parable of the Ten Virgins, as it's commonly known, is a bitter sweet story that Jesus uses to help His disciples see the importance of staying "woke." Jesus says that there were ten virgins and right away he says five were foolish and five were wise. The difference between the wise and foolish had nothing to do with their level of education, the amount of money they had or how popular they were on social media. The difference between the wise virgins and the foolish ones was how well they prepared for the unexpected. There really is so much more to this parable than I could write about in this short devotional. So I would encourage you to read it and study it for yourself.

To summarize the parable, the ten virgins were waiting to attend a wedding banquet. But the bridegroom took longer to come than expected, so they ended up falling asleep. When he finally arrived, it was midnight. But by that time the oil in their lamps had burned out. (In those days the lamps and oil were used to light their pathway so they could see where they were going. There were no street lights in those days, LOL.) The five wise virgins had brought extra oil to light (or trim) their lamps, but the five foolish virgins did not. The foolish virgins tried asking the wise virgins for some of their oil, but the wise virgins said they needed their oil, and encouraged them to go buy their own. While the foolish virgins were out buying oil, the wedding banquet started and the doors were locked. When they got back they knocked on the door for someone to let them in, but it was too late and they missed out.

The one point of the parable I want to stress for today is you and I must stay prepared with our spiritual lamps full of oil. Oil represents the anointing of God. What has God anointed you to do? Whatever it is, do it with all your heart. Love those children, take care of that aging parent, get out and exercise. Or take that course, write that book, sing that song. God has anointed us to do so much, but sometimes we fall asleep because it seems like He's taking too long. But don't get weary in well doing (Galatians 6:9). Keep praying, keep reading, keep pushing, keep your lamp trimmed with oil. Jesus is coming back "soon and very soon" as the song says, so stay woke.

Let's Pray:

Dear God, thank you for the oil of Your anointing. God, you've given me so much and have blessed me with many talents. I want to use them all for your glory. Help me to stay ready for your coming by doing what you've created me to do. I want to serve my family, my church and my community. Therefore, I will keep my lamp full of oil so that when you return, I'll be let into the wedding banquet. In Jesus' name, Amen.

A Call To Action:

What has God said to you about today's devotional?

What things can you do, or what steps can you take to apply today's devotional?

DAY 27:
ME, MYSELF AND I

(Key Passage: Luke 12:13-21)

"Then he said, This is what I'll do. I will tear down my barns and build bigger ones, and there I will store my surplus grain. And I'll say to myself, You have plenty of grain laid up for many years. Take life easy; eat, drink and be merry."

Luke 12:18-19 (NIV)

I was talking with my son Devon when he was younger about how much he was costing me with all of his requests for toys, video games, clothes, sneakers, etc. To which he replied, "That's why I'm never having kids, so I can keep all my money to myself." I thought, *The nerve of this stingy little boy.* But he was so serious. Children can be selfish at times, and who can blame them? From the time they're born, when they cry, someone comes to pick them up. When they're wet, someone rushes to change their diapers. When they're hungry, someone is ready to stick some food in their mouths. It's kind of hard to go from having someone meet your every need to doing things on your own. But that's one of the jobs of parents: to teach and train our children so they don't grow up thinking the world revolves around them. Today Devon is a very kind and giving person who looks out for his friends and family. Thank you, Jesus. But apparently, the man mentioned in today's key passage didn't get the memo.

There's a large crowd of people around Jesus as He's teaching His disciples. And someone from the crowd comes to Jesus with a personal request. I'm paraphrasing now, he says to Jesus, "Tell my brother to split our father's inheritance with me." You mean to tell me he has the Savior of the world in front of him, conducting a "master class" on the kingdom of God, and this man has the nerve to interrupt Him to ask about his inheritance? Jesus basically says, "That has nothing to do with me." And He warns His disciples and those that were listening to guard their hearts against greed. He then proceeds to tell them a parable about a rich fool.

In the parable, a rich man has accumulated an abundant harvest. He has so much that he doesn't have a place to put it all. So he begins to talk to himself about what to do with all of his possessions. He comes up with a plan to tear down his current barns, and build new bigger ones to store his goods. Since he has an abundance of goods, he can now take it easy and just enjoy the rest of his life. While this may sound like a good idea on the surface, the next verse says that God said to this man, "You fool. This very night your life will be demanded from you." I can just imagine the man smiling to himself thinking that his plan was a good one. Then hearing the stern judgment from God that the plan he's come up with will be at the expense of his very life.

The problem wasn't necessarily that the man accumulated abundant wealth. The problem wasn't that he was rich. The problem was that the man was selfish and did not even consider sharing what he had with others. Since he already had so much and didn't have a place to keep it, why not share with your neighbors? Why not donate some to charity? Why not take some to the shelter and feed the less fortunate? No, that man went through the effort of tearing down his current barn and building a newer, bigger one before he even considered sharing what he had with others. When you read verses 17 and 18 of today's passage, notice that he uses the personal pronouns "I" or "my" eleven times in those two verses. He thought to himself—not seeking any wise counsel—*I* know what *I'll* do with *my* crops. And on and on about his goods. And for that, God required his life.

You and I are placed on this earth to be blessed, but more importantly, to be a blessing to others. And while God allows us to accumulate wealth and material possessions, we should not be hoarders. Look out for your fellow man or woman. See if there's someone you can share with. It's okay to store up for the future, but if you can meet a dire need now, why not consider it. In God's rebuke of the man He said, "Then who will get what you have prepared for yourself?" Meaning, you made all these preparations trying to secure your future. And because you didn't consider the needs of your brother or sister, you won't even be able to enjoy the fruit of your labor. Later on in the Book of Luke, Jesus says our lives consist of more than the abundance of things. Those of us who have much should always look for ways we can share what we have with others. And even if you don't think you have much, you can still share what little you do have because there is always someone worse off than you. And when you share it makes you feel so much better knowing that you've helped someone. Don't be a rich fool. Don't be a poor fool either. Life is so much bigger than me, myself and I.

Let's Pray:

Dear Jesus, thank you for abundantly blessing me. Thank you that I can share with others and have no worry about my own lack. I hold true to the word in Matthew 6:33 (TPT), "So above all, constantly chase after the realm of God's kingdom and the righteousness that proceeds from Him. Then all these less important things will be given to you abundantly." In Jesus' name, Amen.

A Call To Action:

What has God said to you about today's devotional?

What things can you do, or what steps can you take to apply today's devotional?

DAY 28:
THROUGH THE EYES OF A CHILD

(Key Passage: Matthew 18:1-11)

"But Jesus said, 'Let the little children come to Me, and do not forbid them; for such is the kingdom of heaven.'"

Matthew 19:14 (NKJV)

I love interacting with children. They have an optimism and faith that is so refreshing. Their views untainted by prejudice. Their eyes unhardened by life's experiences and tragedies. Children are so carefree and hopeful. They're always anticipating the best, hanging on to every word of their parents and expecting that everything will be okay. Children don't hold grudges. They may be upset one minute, but then seconds later can get over their "anger" with the flash of a taffy or an ice cream cone. No wonder Jesus told his disciples that we have to be like little children if we want to enter the kingdom.

All throughout the scriptures, we can see children being instrumental in the performance of miracles. It's their childish faith and undying hope that makes their hearts ripe for God to do some amazing things through them. Let's take a look at just a few of them. You'll have to go back and read the chapters to get the full story, as I'll just mention the highlights.

In 2 Kings chapter 4, we see a widow's children playing a big part in their family's miracle. They were about to be taken away as slaves to pay off a family debt. But instead at the prophet Elisha's command, they were able to participate in not only saving their own lives, but in securing their future. They feverishly helped their mother borrow from the neighbors the jars needed to hold the oil. I'm sure all the while anticipating what God was going to do with the jars. Then they eagerly helped her sell the pots of oil to raise money thinking of all the money they could make. What a fascinating story they were able to tell their friends about the time they literally saw a miracle.

Also in 2 Kings chapter 4 another miracle occurred involving a little boy. This little boy's mother had prayed for a baby for so long. Then one day Elisha told her she was going to have a baby, a son. Sure enough she had a son and all seemed to be well. But then the boy got a really bad migraine and died. Imagine the horror of his parents. The mother went to see Elisha; she believed that he could do something about this misfortune. So Elisha went to the house, went up to the room where the boy was, and lay across his body. The boy started sneezing, and then he opened his eyes. Amazing. I can hear the boy saying, "The last thing I remember was holding my head because it hurt so bad. I came in the house to lay down, and the next thing I knew this man was on top of me." His parents had to explain everything that happened to bring him up to speed. But once they told him what happened, he shared his testimony at school, at church and with his friends.

Then there was the young boy in John chapter 6. He just happened to have two fish and five small barley cakes for lunch. And when Jesus was looking for food to feed five thousand people, He asked the little boy if He could borrow his lunch. Imagine the amazement as the boy willingly, without hesitation, gave his small lunch to Jesus and watched Him turn it into a feast. This young boy had a front row seat to view the power and wonder of what our Savior can do with just a little when we give it to Him. I'm certain he ran home and told his parents all about how Jesus turned his little lunch into a buffet for thousands.

And there was also the twelve-year-old girl whose parents thought she was as good as dead. But Jesus went to see about her. And taking her hand, He spoke to her, and she had no other choice but to respond to His voice. The Bible says she got up and walked, and got something to eat. Imagine her inquisitive mind wondering why all the people were so sad. "Mom, Dad, why so many tears? I was just taking a nap." Clueless to the fact that Jesus just used her to perform a miracle. She was a testament to all her community of His great power. Whenever they would see her, they'd explain, "That's the little girl who Jesus spoke to and she lived again."

Yes, Jesus loves the little children, all the children of the world. Oh that we would have the faith of children. That child-like faith that hangs on to every word of our Father. That child-like optimism that believes the best of everyone, anticipates that all will be well, and that easily forgives. Then God could do some miraculous things through us.

Let's Pray:

Heavenly Father, I thank you for all the children of the world. Thank you for what they teach us about you and your kingdom. Holy Spirit, help me to abandon the biases, prejudices and attitudes that have tainted my heart. Help me to let go of past hurts, disappointments and let-downs. I want to dream again, hope again, believe again—as a child. In Jesus' name, Amen.

A Call To Action:

What has God said to you about today's devotional?

____

____

____

____

____

____

____

____

What things can you do, or what steps can you take to apply today's devotional?

____

____

____

____

____

____

____

____

____

DAY 29:
THE SAVING POWER OF A "THANK YOU"

(Key Passage: Luke 19:11-19)

Then Jesus said to the healed man lying at his feet, 'Arise and go. It was your faith that brought you salvation and healing.'"

Luke 19:19 (TPT)

"Gratitude can transform common days into thanksgivings, turn routine jobs into joy, and change ordinary opportunities into blessings."

William Arthur Ward

Those words ring loud and true for me. I've seen the dynamic impact of having a heart of gratitude and thanksgiving. It changes your entire outlook on life. I'm convinced that some people are stuck in misery and disappointment simply because they're ungrateful. They always see the worst in people. They only see what could go wrong, instead of what could go right. They view the glass as half empty instead of half full. If that is you, I pray you are motivated to have a different perspective on things after reading today's devotional. And if it's not you, but you know someone who is a Sour Sally, share this with them so they can learn of the power of thankfulness.

In our story today, we find Jesus on a traveling teaching spree. Jesus is on His way towards Jerusalem and passes through the border region between Samaria and Galilee. The Jews of that day hated Samaritans and would go out of their way just so they wouldn't have to pass by where they lived. But not Jesus; He didn't mind hanging out in Samaria. Jesus entered a town and ten lepers cried out to Him, "Master, have mercy on us and heal us." Leprosy was a terrible disease, and those who contracted it were considered unclean. If their condition was known, they would be cast out of the city or town where they lived. They couldn't interact with others, or even go near them. In order for lepers to be allowed back into society, the priest had to determine that they were no longer contaminated. So when Jesus came through the town, they stood afar off and shouted for Him to heal them. The Bible says that Jesus *saw* them and told them to go show themselves to the priests. Jesus saw the lepers. He didn't look past them. He didn't cross the street to avoid them. He didn't ignore them. He took the time to *see* them. Oftentimes, we're so busy with our own lives that we don't even see or notice when someone is hurting or crying out for help. We get so consumed with our little world that nothing and no one else matters. But Jesus always saw the needs of others. And when he saw that these ten lepers were hurting, He decided to do something about it.

Jesus told them to go see the priest, and as they went they were healed. The lepers didn't ask Jesus any questions about His directions to them. They simply obeyed Him. And when they did, the Bible says they were healed. I don't have time to go into the faith it took for them to follow Jesus' instructions, but know that it was their faith in Jesus that got them healed. I'm sure they were all excited and overjoyed to see that their skin had cleared up and they would no longer be outcasts of society. But the Bible says one of them decided to go back and thank Jesus. Only one. Jesus had just performed a miracle for ten people, and only one turned back to say, "Thank You." Perhaps he thought of all the normal activities he would be able to resume, like being with family, going to the market or getting a job. Now that he was cleaned no more being separated, laughed at, avoided. What a boost to his self-esteem.

When he went to Jesus to say thank you, Jesus remarked, "Didn't I heal ten people? Where are the other nine?" Jesus may have thought, How ungrateful of those other nine people. I basically just changed their entire lives, and not one word of gratitude. So Jesus said to the one, "Not only are you healed, but you are saved." Other translations say not only was the one healed but he was made whole. Because he went back to Jesus to show his appreciation for the healing, Jesus did one better, and saved his life. That's the power of a "thank you." That's the power of gratitude. When God sees that we're grateful for the things we have, no matter how big or small, He blesses us with more things to appreciate.

I'm sure when they woke up that morning, they believed that day would be no different from the day before. But they had an encounter with Jesus that changed their circumstances for the rest of their lives. But one of them, because of his "thank you," was changed not only for the rest of his life but for all eternity. Because he didn't just receive healing, he received salvation.

Let's Pray:

Thank you Lord for all you've done for me. I repent of the times when I've been ungrateful. You've blessed me with so much, but I was focused on all that I didn't have. From this day forward, I will lift my voice in thanksgiving, paying attention to all of the wonderful blessings you've given me. In Jesus' name, Amen.

A Call To Action:

What has God said to you about today's devotional?

What things can you do, or what steps can you take to apply today's devotional?

DAY 30:
LAST BUT NOT LEAST

(Key Passage: Matthew 20:1-16)

"“When evening came, the owner of the vineyard said to his foreman, ‘Call the workers and pay them their wages, beginning with the last ones hired and going on to the first.’ The workers who were hired about five in the afternoon came and each received a denarius.”

Matthew 20:8-9 (NIV)

I bought a pineapple from Walmart and went to get in line and all the lines were long. I mean each line had people with carts full of items, even in the self-checkout line. So I was patiently waiting at the end of the line I thought would be the quickest when a woman walked past me and said, “Is that all you have, just the one thing?” I said, “Yes.” So she said, “Follow me.” She took me one aisle over and opened the register. All the people behind me started following me to the next aisle. She rang up my pineapple, I paid and was on my way. What I thought was going to be at least fifteen minutes, turned out to be only one minute. I was so happy and delighted. I love those little moments of unexpected blessings.

Some workers in today's passage received an unexpected blessing as well. Jesus wanted to illustrate the concept that one's status in life does not give that person an advantage in gaining salvation. Similarly, someone who has been a Christian for many years does not have an advantage in gaining access to the kingdom over someone newly converted. The parable in Matthew chapter 20 states that a landowner went out early in the morning around 6 a.m. to hire some workers. He agreed with them that they would earn a day's wages. The landowner went out around noon and around 3 p.m. to hire more workers, agreeing to also pay them a day's wages. Then he went out around 5 p.m. and saw some people still idly standing by. When he asked them why they were standing by idly, they said it was because no one would hire them. So the landowner hired them and agreed to pay them a fair price.

At the end of the day when it was time to get paid, the landowner had his steward call the workers in to get their pay, starting with those hired last. Those who started working at 5 p.m. came to get their pay, and I'm sure to their joy and amazement, they received a day's wages. Then those who started working at 3 p.m., noon, and so on. But when the workers who started at 6 a.m. received the same amount as those who started at 5 p.m. they were jealous and upset with the landowner. They thought surely they would receive more money for working longer hours. But the landowner said, "Friend, I'm not being unfair. We agreed that you would work for a day's wages and that's what you received. Why are you so upset that I also gave the others the same pay? Isn't the money mine to do with what I please? Does my generosity offend you?"

Aren't we sometimes like those workers who started at 6 a.m.? We think because we work hard and stay late at night that we should be compensated more. We say, or at least think, things like, "How dare the boss give her that promotion when I've been here longer than she has?" Or "Why did the pastor put him over the Sunday School Department? He's only been saved a few years." Well that logic may work in the natural, on our jobs, or in our churches. But that logic doesn't work when it comes to God's kingdom. My friend, in God's kingdom, regardless of when you started, you're entitled to get the same benefits as everyone else. Salvation and eternal life are for all who believe, whether saved for fifty years or five minutes. And because of attitudes of jealousy and pride, sometimes those who've been saved for five minutes will make it in and the ones who've been around for fifty years will find themselves being left out.

So be careful. Watch those negative attitudes towards others. Pay attention to feelings of entitlement and pride. We shouldn't be jealous when God decides to bless someone. While we may feel like they're undeserving, God knows their hearts and their willingness to work. And He's the giver of all of our blessings anyway. He can bless who He wants, when He wants, and how He wants.

Let's Pray:

Heavenly Father, I thank you for choosing me to be one of your workers in the vineyard. I come with a willing heart and mind to do your work. Thank you for receiving me and accepting me into your kingdom. Help me to never be envious of the great things you're doing in the lives of others. In Jesus' name, Amen.

A Call To Action:

What has God said to you about today's devotional?

What things can you do, or what steps can you take to apply today's devotional?

DAY 31:
NAKED AND UNASHAMED

(Key Passage: Genesis 2:18-25)

"And they were both naked, the man and his wife, and were not ashamed."

Genesis 2:25 (KJV)

Marriage is a beautiful thing. Two people in love, committed to working out their differences, till death do they part. I was thirty-seven when I got married. I had two sons from a previous relationship. My parents were divorced. My husband was forty when we were married. He had a daughter from a previous relationship and a son from a previous marriage. His parents are going on sixty years of marriage. And with all that history, some might even say baggage, there we were, pledging our love to God and each other in front of 150 or so witnesses. Marriage is a beautiful thing, but marriage is also a scary thing, at least for me it was.

Although we had gone through almost six months of pre-marital counseling, I was still so unprepared for the emotional effort that would be required to help make a successful marriage. I am not a very emotional person, and I don't get in touch with my feelings that often. As I mentioned previously, I'm more of a facts and logic person. It's due to a number of reasons, but I believe primarily it's because my past experiences have made me put up walls of defense when it comes to my emotions. And because of it, I was fearful of being vulnerable, even with my husband. My inability to open up and share my deepest feelings, worries, fears and even joys left my husband on the outside looking in, longing for a connection with me that I was afraid to engage in. Afraid because if he knew the "real" me, he wouldn't love me anymore. Because the real me was still insecure, I tried to mask it as being independent. She was still scared to fail, so I masked it as having control. She had never experienced the real love of a man, so I pretended like she didn't need it. Working through all these issues has been a real emotional challenge for me; but I'm sure it was even more challenging for my husband. Thank God he truly loves me and he's mature and patient.

The Bible says that when God presented Eve to Adam, they were both naked and were not ashamed. They were completely open and exposed to one another. No fear of judgment, no fear of rejection, no fear of ridicule and shame. How awesome it must have been to be so very free. I believe that's the way God intends for all marriages to be. If the two are truly going to become one, an environment must be created that allows for the other person to see the worst of us, but still love us unconditionally. As that's what God does with us. God knows everything about us, down to the number of hairs on our heads, and yet, He loves us. So every day I'm working on "letting my hair down" and allowing my husband to love me as God commands him to. If you're married, I hope you'll do the same.

Even if you're not married, God desires that we be naked and unashamed with Him. The Passion Translation of Psalm 51:17 says, "The fountain of your pleasure is found in the sacrifice of my shattered heart before you. You will not despise my tenderness as I humbly bow down at your feet." God does not turn away the broken, bruised, hurt or weak. We can come to Him just as we are and never be ashamed. We can be vulnerable with God and tell Him when we're scared or confused, lonely or disappointed, angry or feeling hopeless. That's when He can begin to comfort us and love on us.

Sometimes we're afraid to be open and honest about things we've done in the past, and it brings on feelings of shame and condemnation. Let me tell you right now that those feelings are from the devil and he's trying to keep you from resting in the love of God. Shame is the feeling of humiliation caused by the consciousness of wrong or foolish behavior. But the Bible says in Romans 12:1 (TPT), "So now the case is closed. There remains no accusing voice of condemnation against those who are joined in life-union with Jesus, the Anointed One." We don't have to cover up in front of God. Instead His love covers us. Read 1 Corinthians chapter 13, meditate on it. God's love assures and reassures us that with Him, we can always be naked and unashamed.

Let's Pray:

Dear God, thank you for the union of marriage. Thank you that You have put husbands and wives together as an example of your love for your church. Help us to be vulnerable with one another. Help us to cover one another's weaknesses and not exploit them. Teach us how to enjoy the love that marriage is intended to provide. Thank you that even if we're not married, we can enjoy your love. We can always be open and honest with you because your love never lets us down. In Jesus' name, Amen.

A Call To Action:

What has God said to you about today's devotional?

What things can you do, or what steps can you take to apply today's devotional?

DAY 32:
HE KNOWS MY NAME

(Key Passage: Psalm 139:1-18)

"For You created my inmost being; You knit me together in my mother's womb. I praise You because I am fearfully and wonderfully made; Your works are wonderful, I know that full well."

Psalm 139:13-14 (NIV)

The human body is a fascinating piece of art. The human body contains nearly 100 trillion cells, and there are at least ten times as many bacteria in the human body as there are cells. The human brain contains about 100 billion nerve cells and fifty percent of the average adult's body is made of water. When I think of the cells, tissues, muscles, organs and systems that all have to work in a well-organized, finely-tuned way, it's absolutely amazing. The brain, heart, kidneys, liver and lungs all working in a cohesive fashion to keep us walking, talking, breathing, eating and sleeping. God is a marvelous God who does marvelous work.

Nothing reminds me of that more than Psalm 139. It lets us know that despite how complex and intricate we are, God still knows everything about us—every little detail. He knows things about us that we don't even know, and we'll probably never know. God told the prophet Jeremiah, "Before I formed you in the womb I knew you" (Jeremiah 1:5, NIV). That's something to ponder. We are not here because our parents decided to make a baby. It was God's divine handiwork that formed us, even before we were a thought. Let's look at some of the ways in which God knows us, according to Psalm 139.

He knows what we do. I remember being a child and trying to sneak and do things when my parents weren't around. Shoot, even as an adult I've done things like sneak Amazon packages in the house while my husband wasn't home, LOL. But with God, no amount of sneaking is hidden from Him. Not even the world's wittiest secret agent escapes God's all-seeing eye. It reminds me of the song by Sting & The Police "Every step you take, every move you make, I'll be watching you." LOL. Yeah, there's nothing that you or I can do that God doesn't know about.

He knows what we think. That sure is scary because sometimes my thoughts are dangerous. I don't know about you, but the things I've thought about people who've done me wrong are not pretty. Imagine God knowing all the thoughts of the billions of people in the world. I'm sure He thinks to Himself, *What have I done? What is wrong with these people? Where do they get these crazy thoughts?* Well, maybe He's not thinking those things, but I sure would. It's no wonder the Bible instructs us to think on things that are true, noble, right, pure, lovely and the like (Phil. 4:8).

He knows what we say. Before we say it. I've said so many things that I wish I could take back. Words filled with anger and rage. Words to inflict hurt on others for hurting me. And God knew about every one of them before I said them. It wouldn't have mattered if I'd whispered them, or if I said them to myself. God knew them even before I verbally expressed them. I cringe when I think of some of those things now. And this causes me to practice being more careful with my words.

He knows our innermost being. He knows us because He created us. He formed us with His hands. Our systems, our cells, our organs, our spirits. He was knitting all these things together while we were in the womb. He knew what would come to be your eye color, hair color and texture, fingernails, your personality, your talents. He masterfully and wonderfully wove all these things together to create you. The you that He knew before you were created. The you that He calls His masterpiece (Ephesians 2:10).

He knows the number of my days. In fact He wrote out my entire life's story before I even took one breath. He knew whether we would live to be 10 or 100. He knew what country we'd be born in. He knew what era we'd be born in. You and I are alive today at this present time because that's what God wanted. It's not a mistake that you weren't born 1000 years ago, or 500 years ago, or at any other time than your birth date. He knows when you'll take your last breath—how old you'll be, what you'll be doing, who'll be around you. Your days are numbered by God.

When David, the writer of Psalm 139, realized that God knows what we do, what we think, what we say, our innermost being and the number of our days, he said, "That kind of knowledge is too wonderful for me." It truly is wonderful. Not only does God know all these things about me, He knows them about you, and the rest of the billions of people in our world. So if you've ever felt that no one "gets you" or if you've ever felt that you were insignificant, my friend, please know that the God of the universe gets you, sees you, notices you, knows you. And He loves you just the way you are.

Let's Pray:

My wonderful Creator, how I love you. I bless your name because you know me and yet you love me. Thank you for forming me, shaping me, and conforming me into your image. When I feel that no one else understands, remind me that you always will. You have done a marvelous work and I'm glad you're my God. In Jesus' name, Amen.

A Call To Action:

What has God said to you about today's devotional?

____

____

____

____

____

____

____

____

What things can you do, or what steps can you take to apply today's devotional?

____

____

____

____

____

____

____

____

____

DAY 33:
COME OUT, COME OUT, WHEREVER YOU ARE

(Key Passage: Mark 8:34-38)

"For whoever is ashamed of Me and My words in this adulterous and sinful generation, of him the Son of Man also will be ashamed when He comes in the glory of His Father with the holy angels."

Mark 8:38 (NKJV)

"Come Out, Come Out, Wherever You Are" is a song that was featured in the movie, *The Wizard of Oz*. Dorothy's home had landed on "the Wicked Witch" and killed her. So Glenda, "the Good Witch" sang a song of deliverance, so to speak, indicating it was safe for the munchkins to come out of hiding. I don't know if this was the movie that first introduced the phrase "come out, come out, wherever you are," but those words were also uttered in the movie, *Cape Fear*, when Robert De Niro said them to lure the man he was terrorizing out of hiding.

In Mark 8:38, Jesus uses what I've termed a "come out, come out, wherever you are" statement with His disciples. He lets them know that if they're ashamed of Him and His words, then

He'll be ashamed of them before His Father. He urges them, and us, to forsake the ways of the world and follow hard after Him. And not only forsake the world, but forsake our own ambitions, wants, lusts, etc., and pursue His ways, His desires, His plans. He asks them what value it would be to gain all the trappings of this world, and lose their very souls in judgment. In order for us to make an impact in this world for the kingdom of God, believers must come out of hiding.

There was a time when I would be afraid and even embarrassed to say I was a Christian. It was because I was not completely sold out for Jesus. I still wanted to look cool around my friends and didn't think being a Christian was a cool look. I was having fun, enjoying the life I thought I wanted, and being a Christian was too hard with too many rules of things I couldn't do. So I was a secret agent Christian, only discussing my faith among my family and church friends. But the older I got, the more God put me in places with other people of faith who didn't mind letting others know who they were and Whose they were. I began to talk more freely about being a Christian, going to church and the things that I no longer did because they weren't Christ-like. Holy Spirit began to give me more boldness and confidence about the things of God. And today I proudly proclaim I LOVE JESUS!

I don't want others to feel the way I felt, ashamed or embarrassed about being a Christian. So if that's you, let me encourage you. Being a believer in Jesus Christ is a wonderful thing. He has done so much for us, even to the point of dying for us. Yes there are things that we should work on giving up, particularly when they are things that don't please God or go against His word. But that's what Holy Spirit is for—He helps us with those things. Being a Christian is not about a bunch of rules. It's about living out our God-given destiny and helping others do the same. You're welcomed into a new family of brothers and sisters who pray, support and encourage one another. You have peace with God and a Savior who helps you when you're weak. You have joy, hope, gladness and strength. Yes there will be times of trial and testing. But the Bible says when we have those times we can still "be of good cheer" because Jesus has already conquered those things (John 16:33).

There is no greater joy than being a child of God. I want everyone to experience this life of abundant living. The reality is that not everyone wants to. But there are people waiting and hungry, searching for something more in their lives. You and I have the answer. But we've got to come out of hiding and be bold about our faith. Tell somebody that you used to live in sin, but you gave that up, denied yourself because Jesus set you free. That's what the woman at the well did in John chapter 4. After Jesus let her know that she didn't have to sleep around anymore. All those nights of her longing for love, having sex with all these men and still feeling empty were over. She no longer had a thirst for the things of the world. She had met the Living Water. The Bible says she ran back into her town and told everyone, "Come meet a man at the well." We too should be as bold. Coming out of our dark places and stepping into the Light of the world. Don't be ashamed. Don't be embarrassed. It's time to come out of hiding.

Let's Pray:

Dear God, thank you for rescuing me out of darkness. I want to live for you, and you only. Help me to remember the price you paid so that I can be free. Teach me to walk in your ways and not my own. Give me the confidence to tell others of this wonderful new life that I have with you. In Jesus' name, Amen.

A Call To Action:

What has God said to you about today's devotional?

What things can you do, or what steps can you take to apply today's devotional?

DAY 34:
WEDDING INVITATIONS

(Key Passage: Matthew 22:1-14)

""Then he said to his servants, 'The wedding is ready, but those who were invited were not worthy. Therefore go into the highways, and as many as you find, invite to the wedding.'"

Matthew 22:8-9 (NKJV)

I love weddings. The beautiful flowers, the gorgeous dresses, the handsome groomsmen, the delicious food. Weddings are such a happy time. Well, most of them anyway. I remember my own wedding day and how excited (and nervous.) I was. Planning for it was a huge commitment of time and money. I definitely see why people hire wedding coordinators and party planners for huge events because they can really wear you out. But there is one thing that gets under my skin with weddings. Couples spend money getting invitations, beautifully coordinated with their chosen wedding colors, pay the postage to mail them out, get the RSVPs back saying that people will attend, but they don't show up. Now I understand all kinds of things can happen between the time you respond to the invitation and the day of the actual wedding. When there is a valid reason for missing the wedding, I completely understand. In fact I've missed one or two myself for good reason. But when you just flat out don't show up for no apparent reason—that's not right. In fact I think it's inconsiderate. The couple has made provisions for you to be there based on your word. They've reserved a seat for you and paid for your meal at the reception. If they're like me, someone else was eliminated from the list of attendees because you said you were coming, so you were given priority. And on the day of the wedding, you just don't feel like showing up. How rude.

I can only imagine that God feels the same way. If you've read today's key passage then you know that Jesus said this is what the kingdom of heaven is like. A man plans a wedding banquet, sends out invitations, folks say they are coming, and now that the banquet is prepared, they have other things to do. Again, how rude. This was the king's son's wedding, so this was a huge gala, similar to Prince Harry and Meghan Markle's. No expense was spared and everything was carried out in meticulous detail. Knowing that you've responded in the affirmative that you'd attend, this was not something you'd just blow off. But that's exactly what happened in this story. Some of them gave petty excuses—I have to make dinner, I have to check on my farm, yada, yada, yada. Others got so angry for even being reminded the banquet was ready that they killed the king's messengers.

The king was so furious. How embarrassing for a king to throw a banquet and no one shows up. How disrespectful. So the king tells his servants to go out and invite whoever they find—black, white, rich, poor, Jew, Gentile—anyone they can find and let them know the wedding banquet is prepared and ready. Surely this was a welcome surprise for the guests. Imagine getting an invitation to Harry and Meghan's wedding from the Queen, LOL. Now the banquet was filled to capacity with guests. But there was one problem.

In those days certain garments were required to attend the wedding. And with it being the king's son's wedding, you can be sure that folks had to be dressed appropriately. So typically the wedding garments were already there for the guests and all they needed to do was change into them. Well one person didn't have on the wedding garment and again, the king was angry. When I first read this passage, I thought the king was being unreasonable. I mean, you did invite these people on the fly because your invited guests didn't show up. And now you're complaining about how one of them is dressed. But let's look at it from the king's perspective, shall we?

The king is God, and His Son is Jesus. God first invited His chosen people, the Jewish people, to the banquet. But they rejected Jesus, made all kinds of excuses for why they didn't believe Him, and even killed Him. So God extends salvation to everyone, "whosoever will," all humanity. The only thing we need to do is accept Jesus into our hearts (put on our wedding garment). Everything else is prepared. But someone tries to get in without their garment (Jesus). Someone didn't think enough of the banquet (salvation) to deem getting dressed appropriately (accepting Jesus) was necessary. Now can you see why the king was so angry? God in His tender love and mercy has made a way for you and me to enjoy eternal life with Him. All that He requires is that we accept His Son. And if we try to enter without having accepted Jesus, God will bind us up and cast us into outer darkness (Matthew 22: 13).

If you've accepted God's wedding banquet invitation, remember that Jesus paid the price for you and me to be here. Let's live for Him and honor Him in all that we do. Let's not make excuses or get angry when God asks us to forsake our old ways and follow Jesus. I love weddings, and it's an honor to be an invited guest to God's wedding banquet.

Let's Pray:

Dear God, thank you for inviting me to your glorious wedding banquet. Thank you for including me in your plan of salvation. I accept Jesus as my Lord and Savior and I want to be properly dressed for the wedding. Clothe me in the righteousness of Jesus Christ, and help me to keep a heart of love, compassion, mercy and humility. I look forward to the eternal banquet I'll have in your presence. In Jesus' name, Amen.

A Call To Action:

What has God said to you about today's devotional?

What things can you do, or what steps can you take to apply today's devotional?

DAY 35:
FIGHTING VULTURES

(Key Passage: Genesis 15:1-21)

"And when the vultures came down on the carcasses, Abram drove them away."

Genesis 15:11 (NKJV)

Where I live it's very common, particularly in the spring time, to see all kinds of animals in my back yard. Rabbits, frogs, deer, groundhogs, turkeys, skunks and all sorts and colors of birds. I enjoy seeing the animals feeding and sometimes interacting with one another. I'll sit by my window just watching them run free and wild. There's one creature that I've seen in my neighborhood but never as close as in my back yard. The vulture. I think I'd almost die if I ever saw one up close. Those birds are huge—at least the ones I've seen in my neighborhood. Vultures are scavengers; they eat dead animals. Their stomach acid is so corrosive it allows them to eat carcasses infected with all kinds of toxins and bacteria. Yuck. But the bright side, I guess, is that they remove those bacteria and toxins from the environment. I tell ya, God can get good out of anything. But back to vultures. I've read that vultures can grow as high as 4 feet tall; weighing between 10 and 15 pounds, and have a 7 to 9-foot wingspan. I will often see them gorging on a deer that was killed by a passing car. Supposedly vultures pose very little threat to humans, but they sure do look mean and intimidating. And I would never, ever try to fight one off. But Abram sure did.

When God decided to establish an everlasting covenant with mankind, He did so through the lineage of Abraham, formerly Abram. Abram's wife Sarai was barren, but Abram desperately wanted a child. So God told Abram that if he would leave his father and mother and follow God, He would give him descendants as numerous as the stars in the sky. Abram had so much confidence in God that he believed what He said. God also told Abram that since he left his homeland of Ur, He, God, would give Abram the land of Canaan. Abram asked God how he could be sure that God would do what He said. So God made a covenant with Abram. At that time covenants were sometimes confirmed by splitting an animal in half and the two parties to the covenant would walk between the two halves. Abram got the animals prepared for the covenant and split them in half. But then the vultures started circling the dead animals, came down and tried to eat up the animals. And the Bible says that Abram drove them away.

Abram was about to enter into a covenant with God and he was not going to let anything stop him. Have you ever wanted something so bad that nothing could stop you from getting it?

Well, that's how Abram was. The covenant was on the line. His hopes and dreams for having a child and having his own land. All the promises God made to Abram were dependent on those animals. Abram was not about to let some nasty, dead-thing-eating vultures mess this up. So he fought them off.

What has God promised you? What has He shown you about your future? What has He asked you to do to prepare to receive His blessing? Do you have vultures trying to eat away your sacrifice to God? Some things in life we must fight for in order to get them. The saying goes, "Anything worth having is worth fighting for." Has God promised you that He'd save your children? Then fight for it. Has He promised you healing in your body? Fight for it. What about that book, business or ministry God promised you? Fight for it. Drive the vultures away. Vultures of doubt and unbelief. Vultures of laziness and complacency. Vultures of other people's opinions and nay-sayers. Fight them off. Drive them away.

Maybe you started off fighting, but the promise has taken so long you've stopped fighting and have thrown in the towel. Well I want to encourage you to "get back in the ring." God's promise of a child was not fulfilled until Abram was 100 years old; twenty-five years after God first made the promise. But Abram hung in there and kept the faith. And you and I have got to do the same thing. Don't allow the passage of time to make you forget the promise. God is not bound by time. Time obeys God's voice. If He promised it, it will come to pass. But we have to keep fighting. Galatians 6:9 (The Living Bible) says, "And let us not get tired of doing what is right, for after a while we will reap a harvest of blessing if we don't get discouraged and give up." So hang in there, keep the faith, stay in the fight. Drive those vultures away and receive everything that God has for you.

Let's Pray:

Precious Lord, thank you for every promise you made me. Sometimes I get weary and discouraged while waiting on your promises to be fulfilled. But today I am encouraged to keep on fighting. I want everything you have for me, and I will not allow any vultures to steal my joy, my peace, my happiness or my faith in you. I will drive them away. I will fight until I have what you promised. In Jesus' name, Amen.

A Call To Action:

What has God said to you about today's devotional?

What things can you do, or what steps can you take to apply today's devotional?

DAY 36:
DIVINE REJECTION

(Key Passage: I Samuel 29:1-11 & 30:1-19)

"But He knows the way that I take [and He pays attention to it]. When He has tried me, I will come forth as [refined] gold [pure and luminous]."

Job 23:10 (AMP)

When I first started sensing that God was calling me to something more and something different concerning my job, I was anxious and excited. But still being unsure of exactly what He wanted me to do or where He was calling me to, I tried to figure it out on my own. So I started applying to different jobs, thinking He must have a better job for me ahead. When I'd hear of a job opening that sounded interesting, I'd submit my resume. I got plenty call-backs and a few interviews. But all to no avail. One interviewer said I didn't get the job because I talked too loudly, LOL. Now I'll admit that I was excited about the opportunity, but talking too loudly...really? Anyway the point is I tried to make my own way to get to what God had for me instead of letting Him lead me. Now I see that the reason all those doors were closed back then was because

God wasn't calling me to another "job." He was calling me to entrepreneurship. He was calling me to a freedom I'd asked for. I'm grateful for those divine interventions.

In today's passages of scripture, we find David having a divine intervention of his own. After fleeing from King Saul, David starts living among the Philistines. The Philistines were about to go to war against Israel, David's own people. David and his men agreed to fight with the Philistines against Israel, but because of David's reputation for being a fierce warrior, the Philistines didn't trust him. They believed David would surely turn on them and start fighting for Israel instead. So they rejected David's help and sent him back to where he was staying in Ziklag. When David and his men got back, they found that all of their possessions had been taken by the Amalekites. I mean they took everything—their wives, children, jewelry, possessions—and they burned down the city. David's men were furious with him because they felt he had led them to this land of the Philistines and now everything they owned and all the people they loved had been taken away. David was heartbroken. But after getting himself together, David and his men planned a strategy to attack the Amalekites, and they recovered everything that was taken. Wives, children, possessions, everything. The Amalekites didn't even have a chance to enjoy what they'd stolen before David and his men recovered it all.

But if David had not been rejected by the Philistines, he would have been fighting in a war and would not have known about the Amalekite invasion until it was too late. Thank God for divine rejections. Imagine how devastating it would have been for David to return from a war he shouldn't have been fighting in the first place and find it was too late to recover what was taken. God had it so that David was sent back soon enough that there was still time to recapture everything before the enemy had a chance to destroy it. Not only David, but his men too. Their wives could have been raped, children forced into slavery or even killed, possessions sold. But thanks to God's timing, none of these things happened.

I know there are times when we want to make things happen on our own. I know we sometimes think we know what we want and we know the best way to get it. But like the scripture in Job 23:10 (NKJV) says, "He knows the way that I take." God knows what's ahead. He sees what's coming down the pike. You and I don't have to try to force our way into any place. God prepares our way, and the doors we're supposed to walk through, He will open them. Proverbs 3:5-6 (AMP) says, "Trust in and rely confidently on the LORD with all your heart and do not rely on your own insight or understanding. In all your ways know and acknowledge and recognize Him, and He will make your paths straight and smooth [removing obstacles that block your way]." This scripture rings so true. In my case, I knew God had a different plan for me, but I wasn't totally trusting Him to make my path straight. I was trying to do God's job. What I thought were rejections from job interviewers was God's way of getting me to His acceptances. God knows how to get us to where He wants us.

So if you're feeling stuck or trapped, and you feel like every door you try to walk through closes in your face, try trusting God. Perhaps He's closing doors to get you to move to where He wants you to go. Pray and ask Him to light up your path, so that you can see clearly where He's taking you. Don't be upset when they say "No." It just means that God has your "Yes" someplace else.

Let's Pray:

Dear God, thank you for keeping me from every door that I was not supposed to walk through. Thank you for seeing ahead and knowing what's best for me. I will trust your leadership and guidance and invite you into my decision-making so that you can take me to places you have prepared for me. Thank you for leading me in paths of righteousness for your name's sake (Psalm23:3). In Jesus' name, Amen.

A Call To Action:

What has God said to you about today's devotional?

What things can you do, or what steps can you take to apply today's devotional?

DAY 37:
THERE ARE NO WORDS

(Key Passage: Romans 8:18-27)

"And in a similar way, the Holy Spirit takes hold of us in our human frailty to empower us in our weakness. For example, at times we don't even know how to pray, or know the best things to ask for. But the Holy Spirit rises up within us to super-intercede on our behalf, pleading to God with emotional sighs too deep for words."

Romans 8:26 (TPT)

Some people would describe the Grand Canyon as breathtaking. It's 277 miles long, 18 miles wide at its widest point and about 6,000 feet deep. A natural beauty with powerful landscapes and intricate rock formations. I've heard people say there are no words to adequately describe the wonder of the Grand Canyon. I flew over it in a helicopter once. But honestly I didn't see too much of it as my eyes were closed most of the ride. That was probably the scariest thing I've ever done in my life. I did get in a few peeks here and there and from what I was able to see, it is magnificent. What takes your breath away? What leaves you at a loss for words?

Sometimes pain can be so overwhelming we can't find the words to express how deep it is. Trials can be so gut-wrenching it causes our knees to buckle. Grief can be so excruciating it leaves us speechless. It's at those times when Holy Spirit speaks for us. When we don't have the words nor the strength to utter them, He is the translator of our pain. The world we currently live in has been infiltrated by sin, and unfortunately you, me, our families and friends suffer from the effects of sin all around us. Whether it's the sting of death, the struggle with sickness, or the wrongs of injustice, we all feel it. I've been there. So burdened that all I could do was cry. The weight so heavy all I could do was moan. Thank God that Holy Spirit interprets my moaning when I don't have the words. And although we sometimes suffer through this life, the Bible lets us know that as children of God, we have something glorious, even breathtaking, to look forward to. Something that our present suffering can't compare to.

Throughout the Bible we get glimpses into what spending eternity with God will be like. Consider the following verses from the NKJV translation of the bible. Revelation 22:5 night there: they need no lamp nor light of the sun, for the Lord God gives them light." In John 14:2, Jesus says, "In My Father's house are many mansions." In Revelation 21:21 it says, "And the twelve gates were twelve pearls, each of the gates made of a single pearl, and the street of the city was pure gold, like transparent glass." Isaiah 25:8 says, "He will swallow up death forever, And the Lord God will wipe all tears from all faces." And in Revelation 7:14-17 it says, "These are the ones who come out of the great tribulation, and washed their robes and made them white in the blood of the Lamb. Therefore they are before the throne of God, and serve Him day and night in His temple. And He who sits on the throne will dwell among them. They shall neither hunger anymore nor thirst anymore; the sun shall not strike them, nor any heat; for the Lamb who is in the midst of the throne will shepherd them and lead them to living fountains of waters. And God will wipe away every tear from their eyes."

Yes, we have something breathtaking and awesome and wonderful and beautiful to look forward to. I know it may be difficult to do because of everything we go through in this world, but try to remember that God has promised us another life after this one. The years we spend in this life in our mortal bodies are only temporary. We have an everlasting eternity to look forward to. This world will decay. Our bodies will decay. Our possessions will decay. But there is a special place that's prepared for us when we leave this life and that's where we'll spend our forevers.

Cry if you have to. Mourn when you need to. Moan when you don't have words. God understands our sorrows and He comforts us during those times. When it gets to be too much to bear, try fixing your mind on things above (Colossians 3:2). Get a glimpse of Heaven. Read about the plans God has made for those of us who love Him and will die in Him. We all have something marvelous to look forward to. Better days are coming. Weeping may endure for a night, but *joy* is coming (Psalm 30:5).

Let's Pray:

Heavenly Father, thank you for the beautiful wonders of the world. But they can't compare to the glorious, bright future you have for me. Thank you for Holy Spirit who helps me in times of pain and sadness. I know that what I go through in this life is only temporary. So I am encouraged as I keep looking toward what's ahead. In Jesus' name, Amen.

A Call To Action:

What has God said to you about today's devotional?

What things can you do, or what steps can you take to apply today's devotional?

DAY 38:
ENCOURAGE YOURSELF

(Key Passage: Lamentations 3:1-32)

"This I recall to my mind, therefore I have hope. Through the LORD's mercies we are not consumed, because His compassions fail not. They are new every morning; great is Your faithfulness."

Lamentations 3:21-22 (NKJV)

In Super Bowl LIV young quarterback Patrick Mahomes helped his team, the Kansas City Chiefs, overcome a 10-point deficit to win the game against the San Francisco 49ers. Mahomes had been a brilliant player all season long but struggled a little during the big game. When asked how his team was able to overcome the sensational 49ers, Mahomes said, "We kept believing. That's what we did all postseason. I felt like if we were down by 10, we weren't playing our best football. The guys really stepped up. They believed in me. I was making a lot of mistakes out there early. We found a way to win it in the end." No doubt Mahomes knew what a great player he was, even if he hadn't been playing up to his potential during the game. And I'm sure his teammates knew the kind of quarterback he could be, and had been all season long. They had overcome worse odds before. Just a few weeks earlier, they came back from a 24-0 deficit to beat the Houston Texans. All that was needed for them to "get back in the game" was a little pep talk, a little encouragement.

No one in this life makes it alone. And when you have people in your life who can support and encourage you along the way, that's a blessing. There are too many people to name who have prayed for me, watched my children, given me money, put in a good word for me and so much more. You wouldn't be reading this devotional without them. I thank God for my village every day. But there are times when you can't get to the village, or the village can't get to you. There are moments when you're by yourself and you need to be your own cheerleader. During those times it pays to have a long memory of the goodness of God.

Today's passage opened with a period in Israel's history when they were being afflicted by God because of their disobedience. The prophet Jeremiah, the writer of Lamentations, spends the first twenty verses of chapter 3 recounting pain, misery and agony. The chapter takes a sharp pivot at verse 21. But what changed? How did Israel go from murmuring and wallowing in their misery to being hopeful and optimistic? They remembered. They remembered God. They remembered God's mercies. They remembered God's faithfulness. They remembered God's goodness. They remembered God's past victories in their lives. They remembered God's promises. They remembered God's works. They remembered God's love.

Most of us don't have hard copy photos anymore. We live in such a digital age that everything is on a thumb drive or in the cloud. I still have old photos though. The ones that had to be developed in a photo lab and printed out on film. Those photos are precious. God forbid something happens to our cell phones or the cloud and we're unable to download or upload anything. Every now and then I go back to my old photos and look at them, remembering the moments that are captured there. Where I was, who I was with, whether it was a happy occasion or not. The camera captured some of the highlights of my life. And just like a highlight reel, I recall God's hand of mercy and blessing upon my life.

So when I'm in a funk and start to whine about how unfair life is and how many bills I've got to pay, and how my children are getting on my nerves—I pull out the highlight reel and remember. I remember the time God protected me from that accident. I remember the time God provided money when I thought I was down to my last dime. I remember God healing my body. I remember God keeping my children safe. I remember God blessing me with a wonderful, loving husband. I remember God always keeping food in our refrigerator. I remember that I've never been homeless. I remember that God has blessed my parents to still be alive today. I remember God blessed me to finish college and law school. I remember God has blessed me with people in my life who will do anything for me. I remember how God gave His only Son to die for me. I remember how God has allowed me to travel and see different parts of the world. I remember that I have eyes that can see and ears that can hear. I remember that I can freely worship God without fear of punishment. And when I remember, I too take a sharp pivot and must conclude that God has been faithful.

Encouragement from others is great. But when you serve a good God like ours, we can encourage ourselves, even if no one else will.

Let's Pray:

Dear God, thanks for all you've done for me. Thank you for my brothers and sisters who keep me encouraged. But I know it's because of your goodness that I have people in my life who love me. Thank you for the memories of your mercy and faithfulness toward me. Thank you for encouraging me with your word. In Jesus' name, Amen.

A Call To Action:

What has God said to you about today's devotional?

What things can you do, or what steps can you take to apply today's devotional?

DAY 39:
IT'S YOUR CHOICE

(Key Passage: Deuteronomy 28:1-68)

"And if it seems evil to you to serve the LORD, choose for yourselves this day whom you will serve, whether the gods which your fathers served that were on the other side of the River, or the gods of the Amorites, in whose land you dwell. But as for me and my house, we will serve the LORD."

Joshua 24:15 (NKJV)

Life is not so much about the things that happen to us, but rather the way we respond to the things that happen to us. We all have choices. And the choices we make every day will determine the course of our lives. When we wake up, we can choose to have a positive attitude regardless of what happens to us, or we can choose to stay in negativity. We can choose to forgive those who have hurt us or we can choose to remain in unforgiveness. We can choose to spend our money frivolously on things we don't need, or we can choose to spend it wisely. Each day, and all throughout the day, we're making choices.

Certain game shows often will have contestants choose between two or three doors, each having prizes behind them.

Without knowing which door has the best prizes behind it, the contestant has to rely on luck in picking the best door. God is such a loving God that He too gives us a choice to make. Instead of making us robots, programming us to follow Him whether we want to or not, He gives us the ability to choose Him. And because He's so wonderful, He's made the choice pretty easy for us. We can choose to obey Him and receive the promises that come along with that choice. Or we can choose to disobey and serve other gods and receive the consequences that come with that choice. But unlike the game shows, we don't have to rely on luck because God tells us clearly in His word what's behind door number one, obedience, and what's behind door number two, disobedience.

Deuteronomy chapter 28 lays out the pros of obeying God and the consequences for not obeying Him. God had delivered His people from slavery in Egypt and was bringing them into a land He promised them, their own land. He laid out the rules for how they were to govern themselves in the new land so that they didn't fall into idolatry. He told them if they followed these rules, they would be prosperous, but if not, they would suffer. And after reading the entirety of chapter 28, why would anyone not choose to follow God? The first 14 verses talk about all the blessings for those who choose to obey God. But the remaining 53 verses talk about the consequences of disobedience. So right off the bat we see the cost of disobedience far outweighs the price of following God. Some of the blessings for obedience are:

they'd be blessed wherever they went, their children would be blessed, their land and crops would be blessed, they'd always have more than enough, they'd have victory over their enemies, everyone would see them and be afraid of them, they'd be the head and not the tail, the lender and never the borrower.

The price they'd have to pay for disobedience was severe. Their land would be cursed, they'd have all kinds of plagues and diseases, they'd never have enough, all of their enemies would overtake them, blindness, madness, confusion and rage would consume them, they would suffer murder, adultery and even cannibalism, they would plant and not reap a harvest, their cattle and herds would be destroyed, other nations would look at them and mock them and laugh at them.

I don't know why anyone in their right mind would choose the latter. God couldn't have made the choice any easier for us. Choose Him and receive blessing; don't choose Him and receive curses. Choosing Him doesn't mean that we won't have problems and disappointment. But we will have an Almighty God on our side who can see us through that disappointment. If we choose disobedience, there will be no one to come to our aid when those calamities befall us. Paraphrasing what David said in 1 Chronicles 21:13, "I'd rather fall into the hands of the Lord than into the hands of men." David knew his God was a loving, just and merciful God.

So if I were to ask you like Joshua asked the children of Israel, who do you choose as your God, what would you say? I'd proclaim like Joshua, as for me and my house, we will serve the Lord. What about you?

Let's Pray:

Dear God in heaven, thank you for choosing me. Because you've chosen me, I choose you. I choose to follow you, obey you and live for you. I will have no other gods but you. Thank you for blessing me as I obey you. In Jesus' name, Amen.

A Call To Action:

What has God said to you about today's devotional?

What things can you do, or what steps can you take to apply today's devotional?

DAY 40:
IMPRESSIONS

(Key Passage: Ruth 1:1-22)

"Choose a good reputation over great riches; being held in high esteem is better than silver or gold."

Proverbs 22:1 (NLT)

There are many quotes about first impressions. Some say the first impression is the lasting impression. People say you only get one chance to make a good first impression. Others believe we can't rely on our first impressions of someone, as true character is revealed over time. One of my favorite quotes is, "If your presence doesn't make an impact, then your absence won't make a difference." During funerals I've heard eulogists say that our life is measured by the dash between the date we're born and the date we die. We should all live our lives so that we are making a positive impact, a lasting impression on someone's life. Otherwise what's the significance of our dash? In today's key passage, we see that Naomi must have made an indelible impression on Ruth.

The Book of Ruth, named after its main figure, recounts a period of time when judges governed the nation of Israel. The

Bible says at that time, "every man did what was right in his own eyes." Although it was a dark time in the lives of God's chosen people and a lot of them weren't adhering to His statutes, one family stands out—two women in particular—as shining examples that there is always good in the world. Naomi, her husband and their two sons had moved from their hometown due to a famine, and settled in a city called Moab. There Naomi's two sons found wives among the Moabite women, Ruth and Orpah. In the process of time, Naomi's husband and her two sons all died. Neither of the sons had children, so Naomi was left alone with her two daughters-in-law. She decided to leave Moab and go back to her hometown. Neither daughter-in-law wanted to leave Naomi and initially both of them were going to return to Naomi's hometown of Bethlehem-judah. But Naomi tried to discourage them from doing so as she didn't want them to be burdened by her. She ultimately convinced Orpah to leave her and stay in Moab. But Ruth would not be persuaded. Ruth said, "Don't ask me to leave you and turn back. Wherever you go, I will go; wherever you live, I will live. Your people will be my people, and your God will be my God. Wherever you die, I will die, and there I will be buried. May the Lord punish me severely if I allow anything but death to separate us."

Wow. What an impression Naomi must have made on Ruth. Ruth was ready to leave her hometown, the only place she'd ever known, to follow Naomi. Stereotypically, mothers-in-law are seen as mean and hard to get along with. That wasn't the case with Naomi for either Ruth or Orpah. Although Orpah ultimately stayed home, she still wept and was sad about the possibility of no longer having Naomi in her life. The pain of separation, however, was too much to bear for Ruth. She was committed to Naomi. The Bible doesn't give any explicit details of how the women interacted with each other. But I can imagine that Naomi must have been kind, caring, compassionate, wise, God-fearing and loyal. All qualities I admire in someone. Most people wouldn't leave their hometown to follow just anyone. So Naomi must have made a remarkable impression on those young women.

What kind of impression are you making on someone's life? Are you showing love, compassion, humility, fairness and integrity? If you were no longer here, would someone notice a void in their life? If the answer is No, then you still have time to change that. There is no greater satisfaction than to know that something you did or said, or just the way you carried yourself caused someone to want to be a better person. Knowing that someone came to know Jesus Christ because of me would be my highest honor. I pray that today, and every day after, you go out in the world and let your light shine in the midst of someone's darkness. I pray that you will be mindful and intentional about your conduct so someone will be drawn to your light.

People have all sorts of role models: athletes, entertainers, business owners, military servicemen and women. All of those people can be great to look up to. But so can you. You don't have to be famous to be a role model. You can be a role model for that student, that neighbor or even a stranger. Be a model of love, trustworthiness, honesty, bravery and kindness. Live your life so that the impact of your dash is felt by those who come in contact with you. Who can you make an impression on today?

Let's Pray:

Dear God, I want to make an impression on someone that will draw them to you. God, allow your kingdom to come through me so that others will be drawn to you. Help me to always be mindful of my conduct so I don't discourage someone from getting to know Jesus. Thank you for being the light in my life. In Jesus' name, Amen.

A Call To Action:

What has God said to you about today's devotional?

What things can you do, or what steps can you take to apply today's devotional?

I pray that these past 40 days have been life changing for you. I know that the Lord has met you each day as you've sought to hear from Him. My time with God, whether praying, reading His word, listening to worship music, or simply sitting still meditating on His goodness, is the highlight of my day. In His presence is truly the fullness of joy.

I encourage you to keep going. Don't stop now, you've come so far. They say it takes 21 days of consistently doing something for it to become a habit. Well now you have started a habit of spending time with the word of God. And it's a good habit. Keep it up. I've found that the more I read, the more I want to read. The more I study, the more I want to study. The more I worship, the more I want to worship. God's just good like that.

I would love to hear from you about your experience with *When I'm With You.* If a particular passage stood out to you, or if you desire prayer in a certain area, or even if you've started a book club, like someone did with my last book, Fire New—I want to hear from you. Feel free to reach out to me at www.firenewministries.org and click on the Contact button, or send an email to firenewministries@gmail.com and I'll personally respond to you.

I'm praying for you and I love you!

LaVon

ABOUT THE AUTHOR

LaVon is a bible study teacher, author, facilitator and speaker. Her love for God and His word is evident in the passionate way she speaks, whether she's speaking about finances, facilitating a women's gathering, or simply sharing the word of God. LaVon has over 20 years in the accounting and tax industry. In 2018 LaVon left her full-time job as a Tax Director to start her own firm, GWC Services, LLC, which provides tax and accounting services for individuals, small businesses and non-profit organizations. LaVon received her BS in Accounting from Temple University and her Juris Doctor from Beasley School of Law, Temple University.

LaVon is also the First Lady of New Mt. Zion Church in Philadelphia, PA, where she assists her husband, Pastor Zan Chancy, in encouraging and empowering God's people to live Godly lives by reading, understanding and applying the word of God. Their desire is for people to be transformed by a sincere relationship with a loving God. She and Pastor Zan have 5 children and 2 grandchildren.

When I'm With You is LaVon's second book. Her first book, *Fire New*, is about how Holy Spirit brings about transformation.

It chronicles some of the ways the word of God has had a life-transforming impact on her life. You can get Fire New on Amazon, BarnesandNoble.com, or at www.firenewministries.org.